I0102593

KILLING COOL

Also by Kurt Keefner:

Free Will: A Response to Sam Harris, available on Kindle

"The Bust of Caesar," http://www.kurtkeefner.com/2012/06/the-bust-of-caesar/

KILLING COOL

Fantasy vs. Reality
in American Life

essays by
Kurt Keefner

WALLKILL
TRAIL BOOKS

2014

Copyright © 2014 by Kurt Keefner. All rights reserved.
Last corrections made August 15, 2014

For Stephanie Allen, the love of my life

CONTENTS

Autonomy does not mean, as is now generally thought, the fateful, groundless decision in the void, but governing oneself according to the real. There must be an outside for the inside to have meaning.

-Allan Bloom

Introduction: Back to Reality

One widespread "meme" of our time is the making of humorous videos using the scene from the German film *Downfall* in which the Adolf Hitler character goes on a tirade because he has found out that the war is lost. People add subtitles suggesting that what Hitler is really ranting about is his favorite team losing the Super Bowl or something else incongruous. Some of these videos are inappropriate, but at least one is almost profound: In it Hitler becomes upset when he learns that Americans call their political opponents "Hitler," thereby trivializing his reputation as history's most evil man.

This video has some basis in fact. A lot of Americans in real life compare their political opponents to Hitler or to fascists generally. Recently, some on the left have called the Tea Party fascists, while it is astoundingly common for the right to depict President Obama wearing a Hitler mustache or a Nazi uniform. If you know anything about fascism, with its belief that violence is redemptive, that destiny focuses on one man who should be given absolute authority, that the state should control every aspect of human life, with all of this wrapped up in nationalistic myth making—then you realize that such comparisons are absurd. The Tea Party may have a lot of yahoos in it and President Obama may be another Richard Nixon, but they do not begin to compare with dictators such as Hitler and Mussolini. Such charges are examples of political hysteria. They are fantasy, not reality, and they are emblematic of what's wrong with America today.

You do not have to be a genius to see that our country is deeply troubled. Solutions to our problems, however, are far more difficult to perceive. One reason for this is that our problems seem so diverse and unrelated. It's as if we're fighting a war with a hundred fronts. Look at some of the troubles we have faced over the last decade or so: the financial meltdown of 2008 and the ensuing economic downturn; the Iraq War and the excessive security measures in the wake of 9/11; widespread alcohol, tobacco and drug use; the dumbing down of education and art; the increased taste for violence and horror in the media, which might be related to our epidemic of mass murder; the never-ending parade of alienated style tribes such as the Goths and the hipsters; political demonization; and the bottomless supply of snarkiness and inappropriate humor that cheapens our souls.

This list may seem like a grab bag of unrelated difficulties too varied to address simultaneously. And we might never even attempt to address some of these problems at all, accepting them as something we can do nothing about. Yet there is a common element to these and many other problems that could allow us to tackle them all at once. What unites these troubles is a way of thinking, a manner of relating to the world and framing the self that has become all-too-common in American society. There are several variants, but the general pattern is an attempt to create a stylized personal reality and an artificial self based on a kind of wishful thinking. To put it simply, we are living too much in our fantasies. (Fantasy is an important and healthy part of life, of course, but we shouldn't dwell in it. The real world is primary.)

Everyone knows about one example of this phenomenon: acting "Cool." In trying to appear unflappably superior, the Cool person buys into the idea that there is an aesthetic "wave" he can ride—a mythic Zeitgeist consisting of ideas about fashion and sociological developments that he synthesizes and then projects onto the world, as if the world had a mood to it. That's the stylized personal reality; the artificial self lies in the way the Cool person "grooves" to the Zeitgeist, donning his real or metaphorical sunglasses and acting aloof. This is not a matter of mere fashion, because trying to be Cool can lead to a number of self-destructive behaviors, such as smoking and drug use. Furthermore, Coolness shapes our arts and manners in a variety of unwholesome ways. Yet we accept it as an inevitable part of our culture. And Cool is just one example.

Falsification of self and reality does not work, of course, since being in touch with the self, the real world and other people is the source of all true success and happiness. Living out of touch with them can lead only to failure, anxiety or, at best, neurotic titillation. Americans are losing their connection to the world and other people and are suffering from an epidemic of hype and role-playing, all because we do not know how to engage reality and be ourselves. *Killing Cool* chronicles more than a dozen varieties of this kind of falsification, from Coolness to extreme religious faith to a modern form of cynicism based on pseudo-scientific ideas from evolutionary psychology. In the essays ahead we will examine these falsifications, show their common causes, and offer alternatives to them.

The pattern is not always easy to see. The disciplines that you might expect to investigate it are all too partial. Psychology might look at the issue of self-definition, but not at society as a whole or at the philosophical aspects of our relation to reality. Culture criticism is good for tracing social and artistic developments but is usually not very good at explaining them. Philosophy can handle the abstractions, but typically is not well connected to everyday reality.

What is needed is a convergence of these three perspectives. Our personal and social lives need to be viewed as a system: Ideas (best studied by philosophy) give rise to a vision of life. The structure of the mind (best studied by psychology) realizes that vision in the individual. Technologies and institutions (best studied by culture criticism) create an environment for the individual to act in that reinforces the ideas, thereby closing the circle. If we put all three perspectives in play, we can see the exact nature of our distorted worldview more clearly.

When trying to address social problems, many people make the mistake of focusing on politics or technology as if they were primary, but they are not: Ideas from philosophy and psychology are fundamental. And arguing about politics or anything else is futile until we get out of our heads and decide to start living in the real world. Reality is the cure for what ails us. We need a back-to-reality movement.

Let me say up front that although I make use of philosophy, psychology and culture criticism, I am not a scholar in any of these fields, or indeed in any field. I am merely an inveterate observer of my fellow Americans, someone who tries to think through his impressions and to put them in a larger context. Readers will have to decide for themselves whether I am qualified to have an opinion on the subjects I write about.

The project of this book is not merely to identify the disturbing phenomena of our time. In every case where I point out a problem, I also suggest a solution. Over the course of the various essays I build up a portrait of a life more free and joyous than the inauthentic lives many of us now lead. I don't believe that we're stuck with our problems. We can redeem our souls by learning to dwell in the world. There is a fount of reason and wonder in each of us that we can draw on to help make life better, if we are willing to work for that goal.

I would label the multi-perspectival and constructive approach of *Killing Cool* "concrete ethics." By this term I mean an ethics that goes beyond general virtues and deals with the specific habits necessary to lead the good life. It's one thing to say "Be true to yourself and live in reality!" and another to uncover the various temptations that lead us not to do so, in the process showing us how to find our way back to the real world, which is our natural home.

Concrete ethics isn't the whole story when it comes to success and happiness, since general ethics is more primary, but with concrete ethics we can address many of society's ills and learn how to touch joy as individuals. I hope you will accompany me on this journey of exploration and growth.

A Note on the Compassionate Classification of Human Beings

Although we should all be treated as individuals, many people fall into more-or-less clear categories. Those types are shaped to some extent by a person's natural endowments, but mostly by their beliefs and fantasies. One has to be careful, though, not to say that the type defines the person. Thankfully, human beings are too good at wriggling out of pigeonholes that others try to put them in for any but the most unfortunate person to be a mere victim of taxonomy. However, if a person doesn't take the trouble to think his way out of whatever box he has fallen into, he may go through life as an example of a character type, with rather predictable patterns of thought, feeling and action.

Killing Cool is full of types. No doubt when I classify a large group of people as belonging to a type, I sometimes over-generalize, catching people who don't belong in my category, but that is the danger of generalizing about human beings at all. It's best to remember that you can't classify a person by a single behavioral trait, that an affinity, a mannerism or a way of speaking is just one tile in an overall mosaic, and that it's the pattern that reveals the type, not a few isolated pieces.

In this book I deal mostly with extreme examples of various syndromes, people who are dangerous to themselves and to society. But most of the people who suffer from these syndromes are not extreme. They are decent folks, and treating them as dangers would be moral hysteria. Nevertheless, I insist that belonging to the categories I describe, even to a moderate degree, holds one back from achieving one's highest potential. We can all do better. My goal is to illuminate the boxes that many of us have unwittingly stumbled into and to light the way out.

Despite the fact that I use a lot of labels in this book, I am very wary of them and hope that readers do not use the categories I set out to objectify themselves or others. I don't believe that people are prisoners of a typology. Everyone is bigger than any category that someone else might put them in, as long as they use their reason, free will and hope.

The Pretender

In the 17th century, Anton van Leeuwenhoek discovered with an early microscope that there is more in a drop of water than meets the unaided eye. What might we discover floating in our lives today if we used the right instruments? Hidden wonders perhaps? Perhaps something ominous as well.

Sometimes what swims unseen is a spiritual disorder. I started catching glimpses of such a disorder when I was a boy in the 1960s. One of my brothers suffered from it, always complaining about having spent more than half of his life (8 out of 14 years) in what he called "these godforsaken little burgs," i.e. the small towns our father moved us to for his work. When I learned the word, I thought of my brother's behavior as "melodrama," but that wasn't quite correct.

All through my childhood and teens I saw the same syndrome like a flush on the faces of many of those around me. People in the 1970s who acted hip or earthy or chic or ironic were almost invariably afflicted. The problem seemed at first glance to be mere phoniness, but really it wasn't, because these people weren't trying to fool anybody else, any more than my brother was. They had just fallen into a certain way of being. Sometimes I referred to such people as "smug," but that wasn't accurate either.

The syndrome I detected during my youth but could not identify was not merely a matter of style. I knew that even then. I spent much too much time in the 1970s and early 1980s around people who did drugs to believe this to be an issue on the order of wide ties versus skinny ties. I saw in my drug-using acquaintances the same melodrama or smugness or whatever it was, and I grasped in some inchoate way that it factored into their substance use, but that was as far as I could go with the connection.

I developed a bad case of the disorder during my senior year of high school. A girl I had loved rejected me, and I had a near-nervous breakdown. I felt empty, and I filled my emptiness with the manners and tastes of a charismatic friend. He would pump his fist and yell "Neetch!" in honor of his favorite philosopher, and he called people he didn't like "pigs" and "rabble." I went against my own nature and became quite cavalier while under his sway. It took years for me to shrug off the influence of my "guru." But I still didn't identify the disorder.

I thought about the syndrome off and on for the following decade, but the next great gelling insight occurred only when I was 35. I was reading an article in the November 23, 1996, *TV Guide* about a television remake of *In Cold Blood.* Interviewed on the set, one of the stars shared a verse he'd made up and forced into the meter of "The Ballad of Jed Clampett" from *The Beverly Hillbillies*:

This is the story of a man named Clutter.
He lost his wife and daughter
Who were killed with a shotgun
That made their heads go splutter.

In Cold Blood was based on the actual murders of Herbert Clutter and his family in 1959. The star's lyrics were incomplete: not only were Mr. Clutter's wife and daughter murdered, but so was his son, and so was Mr. Clutter, who had his throat cut before he was shot in the face. The thirty-four-year-old actor who bequeathed us this doggerel of course knew that his movie was based on factual events. I was appalled that he had made a joke about what had happened to these real people and that *TV Guide* had printed it.

And then it occurred to me: to this actor and to the folks at *TV Guide*, the Clutters *weren't* real. Not truly. They were just *characters* with funny names, like Jed Clampett. And I saw with an awful recognition that there was some nexus where treating reality as a story, lacking empathy, and entertaining oneself joined. This nexus was accompanied by a kind of giddiness, like a fever. I had seen this pattern in many different places, but never so clearly. Further, I reflected that I had sometimes been guilty of it myself.

That's pretty much where my understanding of the subject stayed for many years. I knew enough not to succumb to the syndrome and to cast a wary eye on anyone who did, but I didn't follow it down to the root. It took a lot of writing before I puzzled it all out.

I gave the disorder several names before I settled on one. Now I call it "Pretenderism." When I say someone is a Pretender, I don't mean that he is practicing normal make-believe or that he is a phony, but rather that he is engaging in a specific kind of *unself-conscious simulation.* The Pretender pretends, without fully knowing it, to be a different self, a self defined by its sense of life. "Sense of life" is a concept made famous by Miguel de Unamuno, who wrote "The Tragic Sense of Life" in 1913. It was further developed fifty years later by Ayn Rand in her book on art, *The Romantic Manifesto.* I am using a slightly modified version of Rand's conception.

A genuine sense of life is the sum of your bedrock beliefs about the world, manifested as pervasive feelings. You can feel that life is an adventure or that the world is a threatening place where you'd better keep your head down. You can feel that everybody uses everybody or that we're all vulnerable underneath. You can feel that it's fun to use your mind or you can feel, "What's the use?" A sense of life can be sparkling, defeatist, exalted, down-to-earth, etc., with many nuances. Multiple beliefs meet in the same person, sometimes with inconsistencies, but they tend to add up to an overall emotional gestalt. It's like a tone or mood that is in the background of everything you do and feel.

You develop a sense of life through your pre-theoretic encounters with the world beginning in childhood, through ten thousand impressions and choices that you half-consciously integrate into a sensibility. It is at once something about what you think the world is like and something about the kind of person you are. It helps define you, and others perceive it almost as an emotional "aura" surrounding you, giving you your unique connotation as a person. It is the basis of art, especially music, which embodies sense of life feelings.

The feeling aspect of a sense of life, however, is not a primary—it is the product of your thinking about reality, built up impression by impression, choice by choice. The Pretender, however, is not thinking about reality: he *starts* with a moodlike feeling—call it a "pseudo sense of life"—which he uses to define an artificial self and which he projects onto the world in an attempt to generate a certain kind of emotion or style. In other words, where a genuine sense of life is a *response* to experience, a pseudo sense of life is an attempt to *conjure* experience.

Pretenders play a role defined by the pseudo sense of life they choose. They can play at being macho or torchy, glib or self-pitying or five hundred other things, but whatever it is it will inevitably be much simpler than the complex mosaic that is a genuine sense of life, and this is because it is not arrived at organically. Usually Pretenders just grab it off the rack. They are typically not old enough at the time to realize what they are doing. Adopting a pseudo sense of life is the emotional equivalent of jumping to a conclusion, and like jumping to a conclusion it seems usually to be motivated by impatience with the proper process. It is an almost existentialist maneuver, like a leap of faith in the dark.

Pretenderism is an attempt to control one's experience beyond the point to which one can reasonably expect to control it. Pretenders are often afraid of meaninglessness (frequently in the guise of boredom), helplessness and worthlessness. They project a "vibe" onto the world in order to avoid these bad feelings, living out a stylized fantasy instead of exploring the world and themselves and working through their issues. Most of them see reality as an aesthetic phe-nomenon: for them life is a movie, other people and they themselves are characters in it, and their pseudo sense of life provides the soundtrack music that en-hances the mood at different points.

Pretending a sense of life is an act of magical think-ing, because the Pretender believes implicitly that he can remake himself and the world just by choosing to feel a certain way about them. The Pretender doesn't fully see the difference between the inner world and the outer world. He thinks that his soundtrack music is playing out there in the world instead of merely inside of his head. The idea of an impersonal reality is foreign to him.

Being a Pretender is like wearing sunglasses in-doors. They make one feel cool and they give things an interesting tint, but they get between one and the world and make both seem like what they aren't. They are a mask.

In many cases, the pasted-on sense of life is bor-rowed from role models, such as those in the me-dia. The process is seductive and not fully conscious. Bored children see Bart Simpson and think he's cool and exciting. They get charged up and resonate with his brattiness. They "snap into" the character's sense of life, and before you know it, they're little Bartmen, skateboarding through a world of thrills and fools. They probably don't think of themselves as Barts or brats, since like many of our most important decisions, this one is wordless. Perhaps they think of themselves as "smart" or "cool," but those words are just handles for the pseudo sense of life that draws them. Later, be-cause the child is father to the man, they become big

Bartmen, with grown-up brattiness, and perhaps they think of themselves as "rebels." Beneath this brattiness, however, there is still a genuine person who isn't a brat, with a sad and stunted but genuine sense of life, a person who doesn't know what to do with himself.

Even when the adoption of a pseudo of sense of life is somewhat self-conscious, it is usually still not intended to deceive others, but is a sincere attempt to become something new. For example, as an asthmatic youngster, Theodore Roosevelt made himself over with a program of calisthenics and manly interests. At some point he decided to become a cowboy, no doubt inspired by the glamorous depiction of cowboys in the mass media of his time. Roosevelt's "strenuous life," with its gratuitous killing of animals, crowing over dead Spanish soldiers and calling things "bully" when he was in his forties, was the product of decisions he had made as a child, decisions that left the mark of a child on him his whole life. "You have to remember," said one of his friends, "that the President is six."

Signs and Symptoms

You can often spot a Pretender because of his manner: He is artificial without being insincere—more over-stylized than anything else. You know that someone is Pretending when he adopts a style that no one of his age and education has any business adopting, for example, suburban teenagers who buy into hip-hop fashion. The endless procession of style tribes that have been spawned during the last 60 years—beats, rockers, hippies, punks, hip-hoppers, Goths, hipsters—has been full of Pretenders. You can also spot a Pretender because his manner or work is artificially one-note, as in, for example, the "gonzo" style of Hunter S. Thompson. In the 1990s the favored Pretenderist attitude was chronic irony (Think *Seinfeld*). That attitude abated somewhat after 9/11, but it seems to be making a comeback.

Pretenders leave a wide trail of small, generally reliable signs including backward baseball caps and funny facial hair on young men and bow ties and seersucker suits on older ones, although single signs are never decisive. Excessive make-up and overly sexualized attire are some of the reliable signs in women. People who aggressively act out their ethnicity count, too. Pretenders choose style as their substance with frightening regularity.

Some senses of life simply cannot be genuine. Nobody is really hip or cool: Miles Davis was a Pretender. Nobody is really a sex kitten: Marilyn Monroe was a Pretender. Nobody with any education is really "folksy": Ronald Reagan was a Pretender. Nobody is really morbidly droll: Alfred Hitchcock, Charles Addams and Edward Gorey were all Pretenders. (And I don't think all of these qualities were just acts for the public.) While we're at it, snarky people and officious people are all Pretenders, though not vice versa. Notice that the Pretender is not just one personality type, but is rather a galaxy of related types. Pretenders share a general recipe for falsifying the self, but the particular flavor they adopt varies according to taste.

Think of the distortions of personality that many people undergo by Pretending. Marilyn Monroe apparently painted herself into a corner, creating a role she could not break out of. At the other end of the gender spectrum, Norman Mailer was an example of the hyper-masculine Pretender, living in a world where only the bellicose survive. Mailer's effete antagonist Gore Vidal was just as much a Pretender without being hyper-masculine, as was Vidal's sparring partner William F. Buckley, Jr. All of these people are beyond parody. The talk shows of the 1960s and 1970s were like Pretender zoos. Out of politeness, I usually stay away from living examples, but if you want to look for contemporary Pretenders on your own, check out today's movie directors, among whom they are legion. I don't know about Quentin Tarantino the man, but Tarantino the director is a grade-A Pretender.

Let me hasten to say that most Pretenders are decent human beings and that many are attractive, creative people. I'm not trying to condemn anyone merely for being a Pretender, and I'm not trying to reduce complex individuals to mere "types." Pretenders usually deserve our sympathy, because they generally do not know what they are choosing when they start Pretending and because they are their own worst enemies.

The reader may wonder what the difference is between being a Pretender and simply adopting an "attitude." The two are certainly on a continuum of make believe, but adopting an attitude in the normal sense is typically a conscious and limited tactic for impressing others, while being a Pretender means adopting a manner full-time, unself-consciously, and primarily for oneself. Likewise the Pretender is not simply displaying a persona in Jung's sense or a false self in Winnicott's. A persona is one's social face, adopted to deal with social pressures. A Pretender Pretends in response to private, inner needs. Furthermore, I should mention that the overwhelming majority of Pretenders are not clinical narcissists, although there is a touch of the narcissistic personality style in many of them.

It's comfortable to think that Pretenders are basically harmless, even charming, and not to be very concerned about them. If you don't like them, just don't associate with them. The problem with this easy-going attitude is that a lot of Pretenders are dangerous to themselves and others. Theodore Roosevelt lost the vision in one eye from boxing in the White House (he was nearly fifty at the time). And Roosevelt started the tradition of the crusading president that has led a string of disastrous policies, including the Vietnam War and the War on Drugs. These crusades are born of the disorder of Pretenderism. The political Pretender's pseudo sense of life entails a sense of self-righteous urgency that turns every problem into a crisis—and crisis thinking is almost antithetical to reason. Note that the modern president who defused crises best was also probably the one who was least a Pretender: Dwight D. Eisenhower.

Putting the Syndrome Under the Microscope

We need an anatomy of the Pretender. The best place to start is his relationship with reality. The Pretender sees the world through the tinted lenses he has donned. Typically, he is looking to be entertained by the world, not engaged by it. Reality may not even seem real to him. Rather, to him it seems like a story, all surface with nothing behind it. Instead of seeing other people in a matter-of-fact way, recognizing their humanity, many Pretenders regard them as little more than objects of the imagination to be mocked or romanticized at will.

The Pretender creates a Bubble Universe to live in, a kind of virtual world of idiosyncrasies, no-context beliefs and references to the surrounding culture, all glued together by the story the Pretender is trying to tell himself. The Pretender furnishes his Bubble Universe according to the pseudo sense of life he has chosen: He has his habitual jokes, his favorite conspiracy theories, and references to *House, M.D.* The Pretender lives among these trinkets. They make him happy and reinforce his attitude. There is an excited-kid kind of joy to many a Pretender, attractive unless you spend too much time in his presence and realize that *Harry Potter* really is the pinnacle of literature for him. The way in which comic books, *Star Wars*, zombie stories, video games and other fantasies have become adult fare in the last couple of generations is another sign of the spread of Pretenderism. A lot of grown-ups today are just big kids.

Sometimes what goes into the Bubble Universe is a little more disturbing. For example, I've encountered a number of libertarians on Facebook who compared today's troubling erosion of political freedoms to nineteenth-century American slavery. This comparison helps stoke their outrage, and it creates a vivid image of the state as an oppressive slaveholder. The problem with it, however, is that it is a self-righteous and grotesque analogy that is seriously out of proportion to reality, an analogy that, I might add, undercuts their message because it makes them look insensitive and foolish. In my experience, most feelings of outrage, offendedness and violated honor are Pretenderish self-indulgences, not genuine moral responses. Ann Coulter's theatrical indignation could serve as an example here. The genuine reaction to most immorality is quiet disgust, followed, if appropriate, by a deeply felt yet measured response. Vituperative moral condemnation is more often than not just Pretenderist melodrama.

The Pretender often treats knowledge as if it were trivia for his entertainment, and indeed our contemporary fascination with trivia is a sign of the Pretender's cognitive style. There's no external reality with deeper meanings and internal connections for the Pretender: there's just random, disjointed "factoids." To mention a particularly disquieting example, I recently stumbled across a website that catalogued gruesome deaths of celebrities. That website embodied Pretenderism in three ways: it treated facts as trivia, it treated human beings as mere objects of entertainment and it pandered to some morbid/hateful pseudo sense of life, the exact nature of which I do not care to investigate.

The Pretender likes things that blur the line between truth and play. For many bright people, such things might include *The Daily Show* and *The Onion*. For the cultured set, they could include postmodern art that "subverts the difference between reality and representation," to quote a description that I have seen in the blurbs of many art photography books. One characterization of postmodernism is that in it "content becomes style," which more or less means that reality is subordinated to sense of life. You may think that postmodernism is something you only see in art galleries. If you believe that, watch a Quentin Tarantino movie, and you will definitely see content become style as Tarantino bends genres to serve his revenge fantasies, and you will see a subversion of the difference between reality and representation as he rewrites history to make it more entertaining. Before you brush all these phenomena off as just the usual foolishness, remind yourself that people who get their news from Jon Stewart have the vote and that people who revel in postmodernism are probably among your children's professors. This is a dangerous situation.

The mental furniture in the Bubble Universe includes obsessions with what-if scenarios, "bright ideas" and floating abstractions. The Pretender specializes in way-too-clever schemes that fizzle or blow up in his face, but to which he stubbornly clings. Putting concepts above reality is the essence of a cognitive style called *rationalism* (not to be confused with genuine rationality, which uses concepts to understand reality). Many clever theories from academia, such as deconstructionism, are examples of rationalism. In the world of business, subprime mortgage securities seem like a colossal instance of a rationalistic "bright idea." Modern American history is littered with such "bright ideas" that were probably born of Pretenderism: the New Deal, with its entitlements that we cannot pay for, the Great Society with the welfare dependency it created, the Vietnam War with its slaughter of the young without a defined purpose, the War on Drugs with its imprisonment of thousands of innocent people, the Iraq War with its imaginary weapons of mass destruction, and Obamacare with mandates that may help push our economy over the edge. We keep getting things wrong because of our national Pretenderism. Our mistake is that we are trying to underwrite a vision of ourselves—usually a vision of ourselves as rescuers—instead of looking out at the world for solutions to our problems.

Failures do not teach us the needed lessons about reality, because for the Pretender, reality is not the point—confirming his image of himself is, and that means judging success by intentions rather than results. This is one reason why arguing about politics rarely leads anywhere: The positions we take are often, perhaps usually, determined by the pseudo sense of life we adopt, not by facts and logic or by attempts to find fresh solutions to problems. Before you will be moved by arguments you must first choose to be moved by reality and not your fantasies. Pretenderist rationalism is a closed loop.

Just as reality in general is not quite real to the Pretender, so other people are not. As a result, the Pretender tends to have diminished empathy. He is not a sociopath, but his put-on sense of life blots out the reality of (at least some) other people. A few Pretenders have a kind of artificial courtliness about them, but many tend to be glib and too easily to find others foolish and mock them. Pretenders can be jarringly and cruelly inappropriate in what they say—sometimes without fully knowing it, because they unselfconsciously view other people as mere material for entertainment or self-congratulation, instead of seeing the tangible reality of others' joys and sorrows. Bill Maher epitomizes this attitude.

Faster, Mule!

Everyone knows that the pace of living has grown exponentially in the last hundred years. In many ways this is a very good thing. Mark Twain's depiction in *Adventures of Huckleberry Finn* of river-town men standing around mooching chewing tobacco from each other and hoping their dogs get into a fight is enough to make one grateful for *Monday Night Football*. But the velocity of modern life has a downside. The type of Pretender who has grown up with rock music, TV and computers is often addicted to speed. Look at the explosion in the coffee and stimulant drink industries over the last twenty years and the rapid-fire editing of modern movies and video games. Life in our time is hyped. In his book *The Shallows*, Nicholas Carr suggests that surfing the Internet rewires the brain, making it crave stimulation more and making it able to appreciate depth less. His analysis seems largely sound, but I would disagree as to when the cognitive change began. I would not date it, as he does, to the 1990s with the advent of the Worldwide Web, but to the 1920s with the spread of the automobile, jazz, radio and the movies. These phenomena, along with urbanization and Prohibition's paradoxical glamorization of alcohol, helped give rise to the modern Pretender type: smart-ass, jaunty, faux-sophisticated. (Think Sinclair Lewis.) I am not suggesting that we give up movies or computers, of course, but there are different ways to incorporate them into our lives from the ways in which most of us do now.

Not all Pretenders participate in the general increase in velocity. Many religious, sultry, "sophisticated," or waiflike Pretenders go for a slower pace, and we will deal with some of these types in later essays. The most common Pretender of today, however, is psychologically dependent on speed. His Pretending filters out much of what is nourishing from experience, and in a vain attempt to satisfy the hunger that he has created in himself, he ramps up life into a form of overdrive I call Fast Time. In Fast Time, thought and feeling outstrip the natural tempos of head and heart. Fast Time is the giddiness and feverishness I noticed in many people over the years. This type of Pretender is a skimmer, restive, unable to let anything sink in.

The Fast-Time Pretender tries to substitute artificial excitement for substance. Many of the fixtures of today's life—Red Bull, venti double Mocha lattes, extreme sports, video games, and action movies—are just delivery vehicles for sugar, caffeine and adrenalin, the fuels of Fast Time. Being in Fast Time makes it difficult for the Pretender to concentrate on anything deeper than sense of life emotions—and since wallowing in sense of life emotions is what caused the Pretender to go into Fast Time in the first place, it is a very difficult cycle to break out of.

The Red and the Gray

Many Pretenders have an affinity for gore, as you might expect of people who are low on empathy and who live in Fast Time. Sometimes the gore is real, as in the case of the hunter/Rough Rider Teddy Roosevelt who loved to kill animals and people. Mercifully, today's Pretender is more likely to be an aficionado merely of gory movies, TV and video games, although the Virginia Tech and Columbine mass murderers seem as if they might have been Fast-Time Pretenders.

Gore has become much more popular in the mainstream media over the last generation. Once upon a time, even horror movies were relatively bloodless: Bela Lugosi's Dracula did not even have visible fangs. Now the defilement of the human body by displays of decapitation and decomposition is much more common in both horror movies and thrillers—and not just in straight-to-cable cheapies either. The nadir was reached in 1991 with *The Silence of the Lambs*, which won the top five Academy Awards and presented the viewer with unspeakable mutilations of human beings. Broadcast television now routinely shows things that are almost as bad.

The fan of violence and gore, when he is not simply giggling at the carnage, is trying to have it both ways: enjoying the butchery while telling himself that he's not depraved because, after all, it's only a movie, TV show or video game. This trying-to-have-it-both-ways takes place in what I call the Pretender's Gray Zone, a place where things are neither black nor white. In the Gray Zone phenomena are held in a kind of suspended animation where they offer a frisson of the real without having the ramifications of the real. For example, in the Gray Zone, a person can call something or someone he doesn't like "gay" or "retarded" without feeling like a bigot. It's all just play.

The Pretender's Gray Zone evasiveness only works because reality doesn't quite seem real to him: he feels that life is a story, a joke or a game. Still, the Pretender knows at some level that the goings-on in his Gray

Zone are wrong. Playing with fire is part of the fun. He thinks he won't get burned because he believes that what he is doing exists only in his mind, where there are no consequences. He feels insulated by a layer of irony, and he expects the same of those who might disapprove. If a more earnest person protests, that person will be mocked. "I am above considerations of mere reality," would be the Gray Zone motto.

Most stand-up comics today these days practice their craft from their Gray Zones. Hardcore rap, when it is ironic and not simply degenerate, comes from the Gray Zone, too, but the problem has spread beyond comedy and rap: look at the way the term "bitch" is regularly used to degrade human beings of both sexes, as in the phrase "bitch-slap." America is confused when it comes to ethnic and sexual slurs, and the reason is Pretenderism. Some of the antics we've seen on Wall Street over the past few years seem plausibly to have come from the Gray Zone also, for example, huge bonuses given to executives in foundering companies. Surely somebody knows this is wrong.

Pretenderism, especially in the form of national crusades, takes an enormous toll in blood and treasure. To name just one recent example, the Iraq War seems to have been the product of George W. Bush's Pretenderist desire to be a cowboy along with neo-conservative rationalism about the possibility of democratic revolutions in the Arab world. It claimed about 4,500 American lives and over 100,000 Iraqi ones. It has also cost the American taxpayer perhaps as much as one trillion dollars. Pretenderism has infected the highest reaches of business, politics and the media, and we all pay a daily price for it.

Even setting aside the cost in lives and money, how-ever, I would point to the spiritual harm that Pretend-erism causes all around us. It diminishes compassion, seriousness and wonder, except in the most canned and immature forms, as in the politically tendentious science fiction movie *Avatar*, which tugs at the heart-strings by portraying aliens as practicing the roman-ticized mysticism of American Indians while making yet another tired slap at big business. Pretenderism is a major reason why young people are having trouble growing up: It sets the wrong expectations for life.

The Bubble Universe, diminished connection to others, Fast Time and the Gray Zone are symptoms of a widespread spiritual disorder in our time. Together they characterize an all-too-common modern person, one who does not live in reality, is low on empathy, limits himself to a small collection of mental trinkets, and is as much trapped in his narrow worldview as re-ligious fundamentalists are in theirs. Something has to be done about this problem.

Ending the Pretense

It took me over 40 years to clearly identify Preten-derism. Along the way I have encountered hundreds of victims and dozens of ways our culture encourages it, and I have fought it within myself. It is an addiction that needs to be combated in both the public and the private sphere, because it is an aspect of many, if not most of the problems of our time. I would estimate from my own limited experience that something like 20% of the American population are Pretenders, disproportionately concentrated among young people and public figures. But well over 20% of Americans embrace Pretenderist art, especially music: Many contemporary categories of music, such as metal, rap and country, for example, are Pretenderish to a very high degree. And it's probable that a majority of Americans live in a fantasy when it comes to politics and economics, laboring under the delusion that we will never have to pay the bill.

To combat Pretenderism in the public sphere it would be good to see thoughtful critics using the concept to comprehend politicians, movies, books, and each other. I don't mean the usual sniping, but an introspective look at pseudo sense of life in the political or cultural community to which one belongs. In other words, I don't want to see Commentator X calling Politician Y a Pretender. I want to see Commentator X showing how our system fosters Pretenderism among Politicians (including Y), among Commentators (including X) and among the electorate, who bought tickets for the whole sorry circus. More name-calling would be unproductive, and I am not interested in handing a new club to the ignorant mercenaries who clash by night. We need calm, reflective but morally firm voices of whatever ideological stripe to comment on events. George Will might serve as an example among pundits, whatever you think of his particular views.

I know introspection is a lot to ask, but once the public recognizes that the latest political crusade or crazy art movement or degrading piece of music is born of Pretenderism, it can withdraw its support for it. Likewise the public can boycott or even picket the latest degrading movie. Getting just a small minority of the populace involved could make a big difference. I envision this as a kind of Civil Rights Movement for the soul.

It would also be beneficial if there were more anti-Pretender works of art being made. This could include movies about Pretenders, such as *The Assassination of Jesse James by the Coward Robert Ford,* which was a wonderful story of how a boy adopts of false sense of life based on the media of his time and how it lands him in trouble. Another such film was *Public Enemies*, which takes apart the hype and Pretenderism of the early FBI, in the process implicitly commenting on the War on Terror. I would trade the entire Coen brothers oeuvre for either of these films.

Whatever can be done about the problem on the public stage, real change will happen only on the level of the personal. Fundamentally, it comes down to having the right attitude. The attitude I have in mind is a complex combination of pride and humility. For me, it was best captured in a 1937 best-selling self-help book by psychologist David Seabury entitled *The Art of Selfishness*. Seabury boils his counsel down to two basic principles: "Never compromise yourself" and "No ego satisfactions." I think that as a society we've done a pretty good job over the past 50 years of implementing the first principle: the Civil Rights Movement, Women's Liberation and reforms in the police, FBI and CIA during the 1970s generally have all been about not letting others walk all over us, which is what Seabury was concerned with. (We have started losing ground, however, in the War on Drugs and in the post-9/11 security state.)

The second principle is the one that helps ward

off Pretenderism. By "No ego satisfactions" Seabury means you should not be self-righteous, arrogant, self-pitying, a smart ass, or anything else that stokes your self-image at the expense of real effectiveness. As Seabury states, "No one who cares more for self-glory than for self-expansion is concerned with meeting life successfully." This second principle balances the first: Yes, you can be self-assertive, but you must never engage in posturing or using others to feel superior. This keeps your uncompromising attitude from becoming abusive. Needless to say, we haven't done as good a job implementing this principle as the first one.

Pretenderism is an ego satisfaction, because it puts getting a charge from one's falsified sense of life above living earnestly in the world. Pretenderism takes us inside ourselves where we busily feed our feelings, instead of outside ourselves into open encounters with reality and other people. Ego satisfaction was the aspect of Pretenderism I perceived as smugness when I was a teenager. I have incorporated Seabury's counsel against ego satisfactions into my own mind-set as a standing policy and it has been very effective. Whenever I feel that I am stoking my own attitude and not directing my attention enough at the world, I invoke Seabury's principle and shift my orientation more toward reality. I am now mostly free of Pretenderism, thanks in large part to it.

(I also use another principle to stave off Pretenderism: Whenever I discover some unwholesome behavior in someone else, I always ask myself whether I do it too. Not only does this question often lead me to a valuable insight about myself, it also serves to keep me humble, not in the bad sense of having low self-esteem, but in the good sense of helping me to avoid inflating my self-image.)

I'm not saying that Seabury's advice is a substitute for a fully-developed system of ethics, but I do believe that Seabury did manage to capture two broad ethical principles in a pithy and memorable form that one can use like proverbs to help guide one's life. And no ethics can be effective without wise sayings to make it digestible. Think of the role *Poor Richard's Almanack* played in disseminating the ideas of the American Enlightenment. Seabury's book is about at the same level.

Conclusion

We need a healthy alternative to Pretenderism. That alternative is *authenticity*. Authenticity means not putting on a pseudo sense of life or a pseudo anything—it means acting from a physically, mentally and spiritually centered position and letting life in, in an earnest way. It means only adopting beliefs that make deep sense to you, and it means never "pasting on" a sense of life. The authentic person puts his respect for reality and other people ahead of any attempt to entertain himself.

I wish I could give lots of examples of authentic people you might know, but that would be difficult because politicians, entertainers and other public figures typically put on a performance as part of their jobs, and one often cannot say with certainty whether that performance is a Pretense or not. The last president whom I am reasonably sure was not a Pretender was Gerald Ford.

The best example I can come up with of a well-known authentic person is fictional: Atticus Finch from *To Kill a Mockingbird*, a novel and a film that tell of two siblings who start out as little Pretenders but grow out of it during the course of the story. Atticus, their father, is the soul of good sense and responsibility. He loves his children without trying to dominate them as so many parents do. (To dominate a child is to use her to fulfill a fantasy.) Atticus clearly does not see the world as an aesthetic phenomenon, but as real.

Especially since I cannot come up with any famous real-life examples, I would like to sketch the authentic type in words. Maybe one of your teachers or a friend or your doctor or someone else you know fits the bill. Maybe you do.

The authentic person is reasonable, purposeful and compassionate. He is not hyped or bored. He is present and self-contained, as crisp as an autumn day. He takes responsibility for the things that go on in his head and does not project his feelings onto the world. He may or may not be tempestuously passionate, but his emotions and convictions run deep and true. He raises the Sanity Quotient in every room he enters. His sense of humor is playful and a little mischievous, never inappropriate or mean. Most of all, to the authentic person the world and other people exist in their own right and are not props for his fantasies.

It might be tempting to make a fetish of authenticity and to build a cult around it, with "Hip to be Square" as its anthem and *Oprah* as its favorite TV show. But authenticity isn't something you can adopt directly: It's a side effect of focusing on where you are and who you are. We will look at more advanced strategies for combating Pretenderism in "The Sleeper Awakes," but for most people a good beginning can be made by dropping the dramatics, being open to experience and exploring their environment in a heartfelt way.

No doubt most educated people would like to believe that they are open to experience and that they do explore their environment. But if that exploration gets no further than this week's installment of *True Blood* or support for the latest unrealistic plan from Washington, then we still have a problem. The authentic person will be able to solve that problem by following and developing his natural inclinations, guided by reasoned principles. Building on what's healthy from Shakespeare to the Beatles, he will seek and find better things in both high and popular culture, and in the political realm he will look for answers for troubles in their causes, rather than pasting a contrived solution over a problem as a pseudo sense of life is pasted over a genuine personality. He will be a happier and more elevated person and unlike the Pretender, he will not be his own worst enemy.

I am convinced that for many people, reality is an undiscovered country, full of wonders. Green valleys and rugged mountains, cathedrals and skyscrapers, heroes and wise people are just waiting to be found and engaged. But to see them, to feel them, to let them lift us up, we must abandon the Pretense that stands between us and reality. Fortunately, we all have the power to cast aside the sunglasses, to see the world for what it is—and to become who we are.

As Free as a Finch

I believe that the recent wave of Pretenderism largely grows out of the nature of modern childhood. It has frequently been pointed out that childhood is a modern invention—that hundreds of years ago, children were looked upon as little adults and expected to work as soon as they were physically able. All that has changed. Now childhood is regarded, at least in the developed world, as a stage of life characterized by learning and play, with only a few chores usually required.

Children are natural Pretenders because they like play-acting and because they crave excitement. They spend a lot of energy trying senses of life on for size. But their Pretenderism will hopefully develop into a mature authenticity as they grow up. Unfortunately our style of child rearing hinders the maturation process, in that it is based too much on fantasy and abstraction. We drown kids in make-believe, from storybooks to *Sesame Street*. And we teach children out-of-context information, such as memorized multiplication tables, without teaching them that two rows of three jelly beans makes six jelly beans. Any schooling that creates an artificial layer of abstract knowledge floating above lived reality encourages Pretenderism, which creates a false layer of pseudo sense of life floating over real experience. The child develops an acceptance of things not grounded in reality, just hovering unmoored. (It seems plausible to me that Montessori education, with its emphasis on concretes over fantasy, might be a corrective for our tendencies in this direction.)

Some of our greatest literature deals with the Pretender problem in young people. For example, *Adventures of Huckleberry Finn* contrasts Huck, who is down-to-earth and authentic, with Tom Sawyer, who is a Pretender. But a better example might be supplied by Harper Lee's *To Kill a Mockingbird,* which features three juvenile Pretenders, siblings Scout and Jem Finch and their friend Dill Harris. Probably the best-loved serious book of the last 60 years, Lee's classic manages to combine a story about childhood in a small town with a courtroom drama in the racially segregated South of the 1930s.

Jem, Scout and Dill engage in a lot of make-believe. They get many of their notions out of adventure books such as the Tom Swift and Seckatary Hawkins novels, which play a role similar to that later played by television. When they get bored, they create a kind of theater-in-the-round drama about their reclusive neighbors, the Radleys, depicting their family tragedies in the front yard. The children are especially interested in the most isolated and damaged member of the Radley family, known as "Boo," who is regarded as almost a monster. In the children's little drama we see three characteristics of the Pretender: inappropriate make-believe, obsession with mental furniture like neighborhood legends, and lack of empathy. The novel shows Scout and Jem growing out of the syndrome, largely due to the benevolent presence of their father Atticus, who is the antithesis of a Pretender. Dill's fate is less hopeful. He has been tossed around by life and seems destined to make a permanent escape into the land of the imagination.

(Dill was based on Harper Lee's friend Truman Capote, who may have been the quintessential Pretender of the twentieth century. His Pretenderishness is obvious from his manner, as you can see in interviews with him, but it is also obvious from his deeds. He wrote *In Cold Blood*, a "non-fiction novel" that blurs the distinction between truth and representation in a way that Pretenders love. Furthermore, he created one of literature and film's most memorable Pretenders, Holly Golightly in *Breakfast at Tiffany's*.)

There is nothing seriously wrong with Jem and Scout. It is probably normal for children to be Pretenders to some extent as they learn to use their mental apparatus. And it is definitely preferable to being like the novel's other child characters: a little adult like Walter Cunningham, Jr., a savage like Burris Ewell or a snotty priss like cousin Francis. By modern standards, Jem and Scout are healthy, and fortunately, they have an enormous resource in their father. Consider Atticus' advice to Scout that she learn to climb into another person's skin and walk around in it. This advice is the antidote to Pretenderism because it encourages one to get out of one's own head and see the reality of other people. No doubt the way in which Atticus is always reasonable and never dramatizes also makes him a great role model to his children.

One of the factors that encouraged the Finch children to become Pretenders is present in pandemic quantities now, and that is stories. Modern children, adolescents and adults suffer from an overdose of stories. (And music, too, but that's another essay.) Where children 150 years ago probably spent a half hour or so a day reading the Bible, today's children spend 3-4 hours a day watching stories on TV, reading children's fiction, playing video games (which tell a kind of story), etc.

I don't want to overstate my point. Stories obviously have an important role in human life: they allow us to experience a concretized version of our ideas about the world, and they allow us to try on different points of view. But the over-consumption of stories can encourage a frame of mind detached from reality, for the simple reason that one inhabits the world of the story and tunes out the real world. This is harmless if engaged in self-consciously and with a strong sense of self, one that will bring the mind back to reality when the story is done. But children are usually not capable of this level of introspection.

I am not saying that children believe the stories they encounter are real. Research on whether violence in the media causes real-life violence suggests that this is not the case. I am not saying that children think stories are real but rather something more like the reverse: that children (and some adults) might tend to think of reality as being *like a story*, because stories are where they learn a lot of their basic interpretive strategies about the world. Stories can encourage people to believe that the world has a "tone" or sense of life hanging in the air as something objective, rather than as a feeling within us. Stories can encourage one to think that other people are just characters. Stories can encourage one to think that life should have a hyped pace. And so forth. Movies and TV only make this worse with soundtrack music to rev up our feelings, fast editing and drop-dead dialogue. Whether children actively emulate characters or just tune into the narrative's overall sense of life, they will be influenced by what they see and read. When taken to an extreme, this is cause for trepidation.

At this point, the reader might be excused for thinking I'm a little cranky. How could we deprive kids of stories? They love stories, and they learn from them.

So they do. I'm not saying kids shouldn't have stories. I'm saying that they shouldn't have so many of them (and that they should be good ones). A solid childhood should have some story time, but more time riding one's bike, assembling a rock or leaf collection, building things out of Lego, talking with friends (in person not via texting or social media), reading science and history, and so forth. I also think a little work would be good, too. I definitely benefited from taking care of our yard and gutters when I was a teen. I am not sure whether playing video games has a place in a healthy childhood at all, because they seem to get kids too worked up and because they are probably addictive. I might also add that too many stories mean too much time sitting and too many opportunities to snack.

It may sound as if I am trying to put the genie back in his bottle, a thing that conventional wisdom holds is impossible. I'm not a parent, but I've read that many parents have successfully set limits for their children.

I would limit kids' TV, game and computer time and try to shift their reading away from fantasy and toward something more real. And I would enable them to do other things by buying them a bike or a camera or a guide to trees (or better yet, encouraging them to work to earn the money to buy these things themselves). Scout, Jem and Dill need more activities. They are too much confined to one block in Maycomb, Alabama. It is the combination of boredom and a steady diet of fantasy stories that encourages the children's acting out of the Radley story.

If you know the story, think about what it is that finally helps Scout and Jem leave their Pretenderism behind. For Jem, it is the Tom Robinson case, in which a black man is unjustly convicted of raping a white woman. The injustice of what was done to Tom pierces Jem's heart, and he realizes that other people and their pain are real. This is a hard lesson for Jem, but a good one. For Scout, the final stroke is meeting Boo Radley, the reclusive neighbor, and walking him home. She comes to see him as human, not as a spook, and looks at the world from his point of view. The perspective she gets from the Radleys' porch makes the neighborhood and past events seem objectively real, and not just as a theater for make-believe. The Pretender spell is broken. It is when reality and other people become real to Scout and Jem that they really start to grow up, that they become admirable—because they have become attuned to reality and not just to their Bubble Universe of quaint stories.

I am certainly not saying that all stories are bad. *To Kill a Mockingbird* has been one of my favorite books since I first read it when I was 12. Atticus Finch was a hero that I wanted to be. I had to fight Pretenderism in my own life, but I always had Atticus and his children as models of what was possible, desirable, noble.

Slow Like Honey

So many Pretenders are charged up by action movies, caffeine, hectic music and the like that it's easy to forget that not all Pretenders live for speed. "Folksy" Pretenders, such as Ronald Reagan, for example, tend to live at a measured pace. But all Pretenders have a Bubble Universe that they furnish with the idiosyncratic trinkets that entertain them. They all cast the people in their lives as characters in their private stories. And they all have a Gray Zone where contradictions go to hide unconfronted.

In this essay we take a look at three of the slower types. They are perhaps less flashy than their Fast-Time kin, and they are usually less destructive to society, but they are common enough that our picture of American life would be incomplete without them. At the end we'll look at how to deal with a friend who is a Pretender.

The Queen of Denial

When I was in college I knew a glorious young woman. She was a little on the short side, auburn-haired with liquid brown eyes. She was in a long-term relationship with one of my classmates but she took up later with his best friend, then both of them at once, all while keeping a few guys fascinated on the side. When I told my mother about her, she nicknamed her "Cleopatra" and warned me against any entangling alliance with her.

I didn't have to be warned. I'd been burned before. I made a special point of not responding to Cleo's flirtation. Whenever she made a leading remark to me, I found a way of deflecting it in an ironic, slightly deprecating way. It was a game, we both knew it, and we were both amused by it. It created a kind of *cordon sanitaire* between us that made it possible for us to be just friends.

Cleo had an air about her. I called it her "mystique." "Mystique" was an early version of the concept of pseudo sense of life, but it didn't help me discover the more general pattern, because I only saw it as applying to one person and I didn't work out the mechanism—it was just an impression.

To communicate just what this mystique was like, I'm going to quote two lines from a song that was written about a decade after I knew Cleo. They're from Fiona Apple's ballad "Slow Like Honey," from her album *Tidal*. In the song the singer explains how she is going to keep her lover coming back for more, concluding,

'Cause I'm slow like honey, and
Heavy with mood.

I can't find an exact word to describe this way of being, but "languor" is pretty close. Cleopatra (i.e. the Pretender type, not just Cleo the individual) doesn't live in Fast Time; she lives in Languid Time. Her pseudo sense of life is one in which, not surprisingly, emotions rule, especially love, of course, but not just love. She believes that she has great emotional insight and empathy, but, actually, however, she can be quite obtuse and is often capable of just a few stereotyped feelings. Cleopatra often believes in something like Jungian psychology with its archetypes, or in less educated instances of the type, possibly astrology—some esoteric insight into character. In addition she tends to come up with fantasy analyses of people around her, such as So-and-So is a Heathcliff. Romanticism, in the sense of unrealistic fantasies, is part of her Bubble Universe. She can be quite reasonable in some ways, but this is due to her skill at compartmentalizing her life.

Although you might expect her to, Cleopatra doesn't necessarily read a lot of romances. She prefers books that play to her sense of emotional intuition, like those of Herman Hesse. She also likes psychology, self-help and sometimes occult books. There is an aspect of the tragic to many Cleopatras. They often have a sense of foreboding and of being trapped. I suspect that many of them received unwanted male attention at too young an age and that they learned how to handle people (i.e. men) by behaving seductively, and that as adults they feel the confinement of this way of life. Most Cleopatras have a lot of male "friends" and very few female.

Cleopatra doesn't have normal empathy. Since women almost don't exist for her, she doesn't have much feeling for them. She largely sees men, not as sex objects exactly, but as vehicles for reaffirming her self-worth via romance (and sex, if necessary). Another Cleopatra I knew in college, when I once made a gallant gesture to her, informed me that I might get to be one of her "knights." This sent a shudder through me, as I envisioned a group of men eagerly waiting on her, and I started distancing myself from her after that.

Cleopatra, like other Pretenders, assigns people roles in her fantasies. Most of these roles have to do with men competing for her attention. This is of course using people, but it is not entirely unfair to the men in her life to use them, because they are desperate for her affection and do not even try to see her as she is. At some point she tires of the drama and entertains dreams of innocence, of playing on the beach with children. She longs for relief from the pressure she feels from men all the time (which she largely invites). My friend Cleo in college surely knew that sleeping with her boyfriend and his best friend at the same time was wrong, but she kept that thought in her Gray Zone and didn't confront it. College dorms are pressure cookers, and there was no escape for her.

If you want a well-known example of a Cleopatra, you might look at Marilyn Monroe. It's hard to separate what in Monroe's manner was self-deceptive Pretension and what was a performance for the fans, but she does at least appear to fit into the Cleopatra category. Unfortunately, she seems to have trapped herself in her part, and she ultimately committed suicide. It is irresistible to speculate that if she had had more female friends and fewer lovers, she might have had someone to turn to in her hour of despair.

Many people love Monroe, even 50 years after

her death. I don't. Although I think she was beautiful in photographs, whenever I see footage of her, I just think that nobody could genuinely be that sexualized, and that to know such a woman in person would be unbearable. She was so obviously not authentic, and her Pretense veered between manipulative and pathetic. Thinking that she was sexy would be like being amused by one of those really neurotic stand-up comics. The pathology just spoils the pleasure.

This, by the way, is what happens when you take people seriously. You have to make an extra effort to find good people to admire, because if you choose to look, you can see that many of the standard idols are clay up to the waist. At the very least you have to find more adult ways to admire them, taking into account their realities and not treating them as uncomplicated heroes. People who love Monroe need to lose the infatuation with the Hollywood ideal, which not only abuses women but which is *simply not real.* Some of Monroe's admirers want it both ways: they want to worship her glamour while wallowing in her tragedy. But lamenting the tragedy should make them loathe the idea of the glamour that helped lead to the tragedy. This contradiction comes from their Gray Zone, of course.

I'd like to propose an antithesis for Cleopatra. It's tough, because she might need psychiatric help and not just advice from a friend or a book (especially if she was sexually abused as a girl by her father). At the very least I would try to get her away from men she could get involved with. Send her off with other women on a retreat and see whether she can learn something. Don't let her spend time around old people, children, little animals or anything she can pity and identify with. Who she needs to identify with are *other women*, because, paradoxically, for all her feminine trappings, she doesn't know how to be a woman, just a little girl who tries to get Daddy's attention by being his princess.

The best outcome for Cleopatra might be finding a man who loves her without being enthralled by her charms, who sees through her and gently nudges her when she starts to let the honey flow. This ideal man doesn't play games, so she can trust him and stop acting seductive. This might be the best possible outcome, since Cleopatra will probably always be a man-centered woman.

I believe encouragement and guidance from people in her life can make a difference to Cleopatra, but ultimately if she is to change she needs to get counseling or to make a firm decision to challenge the fundamentals of her life, or both. But then, you could say that about a lot of people.

Elves in the Starlight

Another character type that came into its own in the nineteenth century and still thrives today is one I call the Dreamy Pretender. This type, with many variants, is mostly found among girls and women and is characterized by Romantic wistfulness and a love of mood and atmosphere. The Dreamy Pretender type overlaps with Cleopatra but is usually less concerned with the opposite sex and more concerned with the pleasures of consuming—and sometimes making—art and style. A sense of refinement, usually a bit strained, pervades this Pretender's feelings for Tennyson's poetry and pre-Raphaelite paintings (nineteenth-century version), and *Edward Scissorhands* and A.S. Byatt's *Possession* (twentieth-century version). One could also include the Goth sensibility as well as the misty mystic Celtic New Age esthetic that unites Led Zeppelin and Enya. Much of our culture's fascination with fantasy and the macabre comes from this impulse, and it sometimes merges with a kind of morbid drollness, as in *The Addams Family* and Edward Gorey. Many or most of the teenage girls who swoon for the *Twilight* books and movies are no doubt Dreamy Pretenders, as well.

I don't have a really good example of a famous Dreamy Pretender. Performers such as Stevie Nicks and Loreena McKennitt embody the type in their on-stage personae, but I have no idea what they are like offstage and don't believe that it is appropriate to speculate. The actress Winona Ryder has made something of a career playing Dreamers in the movies.

A paradigmatic example of the Dreamy Pretender pseudo sense of life can be found in Don McLean's 1971 song "Vincent," with its climactic line "This world was never meant for one as beautiful as you." That line is almost the motto of the Dreamy Pretender, with its depiction of a heart too sensitive for the rough and tumble of human society. The best visual representation of Dreaminess is probably Waterhouse's painting "The Lady of Shalott," inspired by a poem by Tennyson about a woman with a beautiful tragic face in a boat drifting downriver to her doom.

Instead of the typical Pretender's Fast Time or

Cleopatra's Languid Time, the Dreamy Pretender has Atmospheric Time, where the picturesque and moody aspects of life are emphasized and relished. The Dreamer's slower sensibility is a refreshing change from the hectic pace of the Fast-Time Pretender, but it still filters out nourishing elements of reality—for example, brisk and crisp rationality. Many Dreamers are mystics, at least as far as their aesthetics go, if not religiously.

The Bubble Universe is every bit as well-stocked among Dreamy Pretenders as among Fast-Time Pretenders. Some varieties of Dreamy Pretender embrace self-pitying myths about the meanness of the world and the specialness of herself. This idea of specialness is usually not narcissistic. Rather, her fantasies of being special are often a defensive reaction to mistreatment at the hands of brutish family members or bullying classmates. In any case, Dreamy Pretenders are lost in fantasy. Once upon a time, it was stories of castles and maidens; now it is tales of vampires or werewolves. Unfortunately, some Dreamers in recent decades have been embracing various forms of paganism such as Wicca. It has always amazed me that people who are smart enough to escape from Christianity are gullible enough to fall for a 60-year old phony pagan "religion." But then for Pretenders reality is not the point; reaffirming one's pseudo sense of life is.

Most Pretenders have a problem with empathy. In the case of the Dreamy Pretender, the problem is somewhat ameliorated because she is so sensitive to suffering, her own and others'. As such she can be quite sympathetic. However, she has a tendency to fetishize suffering, to wallow in it and to make a self-serving narrative out of it. For that reason, getting sympathy from a Dreamy Pretender is a mixed blessing. It's nice to have one's feelings be heard by others, but not so nice to be pitied or caught up in someone else's epic tragedy. Those sufferers who do want a place in her heartrending tale are usually Pretenders themselves, and when such a person links up with a Dreamer, what results is a little Pretender *pas de deux*. An example of this would be those pairs of Goth friends you see in high schools sometimes, the kind that make you cringe as they walk by because you're afraid they're working on a suicide pact. The Gray Zone in some Dreamy Pretenders is quite well developed as they sometimes feel that their lifelong suffering entitles them to favor themselves unfairly. Feelings trump justice, in pretty much all Pretenders.

There are several kinds of Dreamy Pretenders, but each has a consistent underlying pattern. She is much more likely to go in for poetry or "meaningful" song lyrics than most other people. Depending on her intelligence, education and sophistication, she prefers romantic poets such as Rod McKuen or John Keats to harder-edged bards such as John Donne or T.S. Eliot. She goes in for a waiflike or melancholy style of filmmaking, rather than the more common hit-you-over-the-head style of today. Her preferred films might be *The Nightmare Before Christmas* or *Amélie*. Faves among musical acts could include Delerium (sic) or The Cure (sick). Clothing tends to communicate flowing emotions à *la* Stevie Nicks or a Goth style of gauzy mourning.

Of course, Dreamy Pretenders usually grow out of their Pretense to some extent. Women in their thirties and beyond rarely dress all in black and moon around their bedrooms. Sometimes Pretenderism is a just a phase, perhaps even a necessary one, that people pass through. But very often it fuses with one's personality. Then it becomes muted but still is present. I've known people in their fifties and sixties who were Pretenders, although they were usually much smoother about it than their younger kin.

The Dreamy Pretender is more multi-media than the typical person. Like most folks she likes the electric media and novels, but she also cares for poetry, paintings, tarot cards and collages. Art plays a bigger role in her life than it does for most people today; she is sort of a bizarre throwback to higher culture, as it existed in the nineteenth century. If she parlays her interest in the arts into something more serious, such as scholarship or making her own good art, then her Dreamy Pretender phase could turn out to have been beneficial to her. Sadly, Dreaminess is more often an excuse for self-indulgent non-achievement, since self-pity is the enemy of ambition.

I think the core problem of the Dreamer is that she feels helpless in the face of an oppressive social environment, and she is trying to express her individuality in a kind of passive-dramatic way. If I were going to give her advice it would be, "You're not stuck in this place you don't like. You can escape when you're 18, or even sooner if necessary. You can find a world where you don't have to be defensive. Don't carry your family or your high school around on your back. They don't define you. Take your interesting interests and follow up on them. Don't wallow in them—see where they came from—see where they go. Look for their complements. Challenge yourself, because the biggest determining factor in your life is you. Merely reacting to others, no matter how serious the provocation, is the kiss of death."

The Rules of Attraction

All versions of the Pretender believe at some level that wishing makes it so insofar as they are trying to wish the universe into having the kind of "tone" they want it to have. But our next Pretender takes the belief to an extreme. She believes, more of less explicitly, that the universe will mold itself to her desires, at least if she thinks about them the right way. This type is encouraged by the "New Thought" religious movement and by self-help books such as Napoleon Hill's 1937 "classic" *Think and Grow Rich* and Rhonda Byrne's 2006 film-into-book *The Secret.* All of these sources claim that we can change the outcomes in our lives simply by changing our thinking. Byrne, for example, believes in the so-called "Law of Attraction," whereby good thoughts attract good outcomes, as magnets attract iron. Taking a positive attitude toward one's endeavors is a good thing of course, but the real heavy lifting of affecting outcomes in the world comes from understanding reality and acting in it, neither of which the positive-thinking crowd encourages very much.

The Law of Attraction has become a chillingly widespread idea. I know people from as far away as Kenya and Saudi Arabia who say that they believe in it. We might call the Pretender type who follows the Law of Attraction the "Pollyanna," after the title character of Eleanor Porter's 1913 novel. The Pollyanna has an attitude of Pretended optimism. Pollyannas march through life with a fixed smile on their lips. The real world is so heavily filtered by their proverbs and rationalizations that they can barely be said to see it at all. They believe, at least implicitly, in a philosophical premise that Ayn Rand called the Primacy of Consciousness, which holds that consciousness gives rise to reality, rather than the other way around. They believe their attitude can make the world over, at least their part of it. All the types in this book who falsify themselves and reality hold this premise, too, just to a lesser degree. The opposite premise is called the Primacy of Existence, and it is a reality-centered approach to living. We will discuss both premises at length later.

Polllyannas have a problem when they don't get what they want, because if the law of attraction is valid, such a thing should not be possible. When it happens, they tend to resort to one of a number of rationalizations to lessen the cognitive dissonance: 1. What I want will still come, just later. 2. I didn't want it hard enough. 3. I really needed something else and God/the universe/my oversoul sent me that instead. 4. What I got in this life I actually chose when I was between lives so that in a larger sense I did get what I want. In any case, every frustration leads the Pollyanna to burrow more deeply into the claustrophobic chambers of her mind, never admitting her frustration.

I know it sounds as if I am making this up—that nobody could be this out of touch with reality, but 19 million people have bought Byrne's book.

Although the Pollyanna is fairly consistent in his or her Pretended sense of life (sunny but rigid)—I haven't observed a consistent pace in Pollyannas   I'm not sure there is a pattern here. There is a clear pattern in other areas, however. Their whole lives are Bubble Universes, and their empathy is limited by the fact that they live so completely in their heads. At the same time, they tend not to be malicious people, so their lack of empathy does not usually lead them to harm others, at least not intentionally.

A real-life example of the Pollyanna might be Michael Jackson, who even dubbed his ranch Neverland, in honor of that fictional Pollyanna, Peter Pan. Jackson, if the stories about him are true, did harm others, although I suspect he took an infantile rather than a sadistic attitude toward his alleged victims. But his worst victim may have been Michael Jackson, whom he vainly struggled to wish into being a white man. (Thanks to Dr. Judith Price of *The Huffington Post* for this example.)

Can Pollyanna be saved? I have been trying to propose some kind of solution to every problem I identify, but, honestly, I can't think of one here. If you don't let reality in, then how can anything change you? Pollyannas and some religious Pretenders live in what amounts to a closed system. And they might never break out of it. Their best hope might be that they someday get tired of the Pretense, but I don't think that very likely. I've seen a Pollyanna hit bottom and come up Pretending some more. I'm not sure they can learn.

Dealing with Pretenders

There are of course many more types of Pretender than the ones I have described. They don't always fall into neat categories, either: A woman of my acquaintance in her sixties is part Cleopatra, part Dreamer and part Pollyanna. The Pretender, of whatever variety, is practicing some form of self-deception, but one that is mostly or entirely unselfconscious and is therefore not usually immoral (except when it involves outright cruelty).

I feel sorry for the Cleopatras, Dreamers and Pollyannas of this world. Where most Pretenders are largely trying to entertain themselves, this trio seems more like they're trying to escape something bad. What is wrong with them seems less like a character flaw and more like a defense mechanism.

I'm not saying we should tiptoe around Pretenders as if they were mentally disturbed. Most Pretenders are charming and funny and can be good to pal around with. However, we cannot take Pretenders at face value when we talk to them. The Pretender has a hidden agenda, hidden even from himself most of the time. Usually that doesn't matter much, because it is not one's job to go around trying to "fix" people. But sometimes you do want to say something. Then your attitude should be to take the Pretender seriously, in fact more seriously than he probably takes himself. Don't confront a Pretender with your "diagnosis" of him; just make your knowledge of his habit the unseen presence in the room. Address specific elements of his Pretenderism that seem to be a problem: Casually remind him when he makes a joke about somebody's pain, that that person has feelings, too. When he gets rationalistic, try to bring him down to earth. When he zooms along in Fast Time, hook his attention and say "Let's dial it back a notch." If you are on good enough terms with him, you might occasionally say, "Hey, remember this isn't all in your head." Don't lecture; be a foil.

It is my impression that except for Pollyannas and the seriously religious, most people would like to live more in reality, if they can do so without feeling meaningless, helpless or worthless. Your job when you deal with Pretenders, is to show by example and, where appropriate, by exhortation how this is possible. If they "get it" and choose to do something it about it, you may get to witness something truly beautiful: the birth of an authentic adult human being.

Sex and Power, Hugs and Wonder

The two American films that were the biggest game-changers of the last 50 years were *The Godfather*, which spawned a wave of films that featured criminals as protagonists, and *Star Wars*, which gave rise to a string of science fiction epics. Gangster movies and science fiction are the poles of big-budget American cinema, the archetypes that many other movie genres follow. What does the popularity of these categories of film tell us about ourselves?

Gangster movies have been with us since at least the 1930s, but *The Godfather* in 1972 started a new era of epic stories about thieves and killers, giving rise to a kind of "criminal chic." Highlights would include *Scarface, Goodfellas, Reservoir Dogs, Pulp Fiction*, along with TV series such as *The Sopranos* and *Boardwalk Empire,* but there are many, many others. The characters in these stories value money (without achievement), dominance over others, and usually, casual sex. Most of the characters in these stories are not thinking men, like the Machiavellian criminals in *The Godfather*. In fact, they seem determined to show that one can get through life without any serious thinking, just acting on impulse and "instinct." There can be no doubt that most of these stories glamorize criminals, even if they sometimes wear a little "crime does not pay" fig leaf. The audience is supposed to enjoy the audacity of the hard man, his machismo, his earthiness.

Why do people respond positively to these violent films about violent men? I think the main reason is that many people believe that these movies are *right* about life, at least symbolically: they feel that life really is all about clawing your way to the top in a struggle for survival and that you should take your pleasures along the way. If you're smart, you'll be calculating about it, but a real man is more or less a wolf—a predator among rivals and prey. This is a view that is not restricted to movies about gangsters. You can see it in the film *Wall Street* and in the American version of *House of Cards,* and in many other movies and TV shows. Other stories about hard men do not feature criminals, but warriors, gladiators or action heroes, sometimes honorable, sometimes not, but always violent. There's a fine line between these categories. The most recent standout example has to be *Game of Thrones.*

Science fiction and fantasy point toward a different way of thinking. Although both genres can be quite dark, they usually have" nice" protagonists such as Harry Potter and Luke, Leia and Han from *Star Wars.* These people are interested in freedom and exploration. Brutality and sexuality in most science fiction stories are kept to a minimum, although bloodless ray-gun battles are plentiful. Some science fiction is about the survival of the fittest, such as *Alien* and *Predator,* but such stories are thematically often more like action movies than like science fiction at its best and purest. Archetypal science fiction and fantasy necessarily elicits wonder and fires the imagination, even at its dystopian darkest. But where crime shows give us the picture of man as a violent animal, science fiction usually offers up a representation of human beings as curious and childlike people or aliens, albeit ones who sometimes have to fight for their freedom or their lives.

So what do these genres of film and TV show us about our national character? Well, we have to be careful here. Someone can like *The Sopranos* without being crude or *Star Wars* without being infantile. I like both myself. You cannot "diagnose" a character type from one or two preferences. But liking these movies can be part of larger patterns of thought, which can be "diagnosed" with enough evidence.

To understand these patterns we have to look at how the people involved view values. Among the character types we are considering values are not thought to be developed through a process of reason but are considered to be inborn like an animal's or a child's. Although the animal and child variants are superficially quite different, I believe it makes sense to treat them as a single, cloudlike entity. I call the overarching idea "primalism," because it holds that our values are largely "primal," i.e. preset, rather than developed rationally. According to primalism, we just "naturally" crave things like hot sex with strangers (because we are basically animals) or warm hugs with strangers (because we are basically children).

Originally, these two perspectives on humanity were combined in the Christian model of the person, which held that the redeemed soul is like a child, but that it is tethered to a body that is like an untamed animal. Modern thought split this model into two parts: Hard science claimed the body, while the humanities and more humanistic social sciences claimed the attributes of the soul, if not the supernatural entity itself. Note that what is largely missing from the original Christian model and from its two modern fragments is reason. Yes, one might use reason to do science and clarify one's values, but one's values are not themselves to any significant extent the product of reason. We just want what it is in our nature to want.

Primalism is an extremely widespread phenomenon in American life. Many people believe in the survival of the fittest and many others believe that love conquers all. Although a pure primalist of either variety would be pathological, many people buy into some portion of the idea, while remaining largely functional. You may wonder why you have never heard of primalism up to now. That's because there is no primalist "brand" in philosophy and psychology: Primalism is a nebulous set of beliefs in popular consciousness growing out of the convergence and dumbing down of a collection of related theories from science and philosophy, as realized in the mass media and individual desires. It has more of a literary coherence than an abstract unity.

As the various theories that give rise to primalism get sifted through the culture, people develop immature fantasies about being virile and fierce, or about being inquisitive and sweet. They buttress these fantasies with idols from the media like Ah-nold Schwarzenegger or Yoda and with slogans like "Only the strong survive," or "All you need is love," building up what I call a "fantasy complex" out of hand-me-down beliefs, media role models and adolescent fantasies. This complex of sticky dribs and scraps is the form philosophy takes in most people's lives, since very few people actually think through the explicit logic of ideas in any detail.

The animal primalist feels effective because he's aggressive (at least in his speech and fantasies), while the child primalist feels enlightened because she's loving and/or open to the universe (at least in the things she watches and reads). But each is a Pretender, grooving on his or her pseudo sense of life feelings of being tough or curious as the case may be. But each is a special kind of Pretender, because rather than putting on just a feeling, each adopts an ideology, in the form of bumper stickers and movie clips and usually just enough theory to confirm his or her biases. Like other Pretenders, the primalists are jumping to an emotional conclusion, but unlike most other Pretenders, they are usually jumping to intellectual conclusions, too.

Primalism is not good for the primalist, nor is it good for society. To beat it back, we need to expose its presuppositions while offering some hints as to the proper relationship of reason and values.

We could compare primalism to a Venn diagram made of two overlapping clouds. The animal primalist cloud contains such values as survival, illicit sex, status, power, territory, money, etc. The child primalist cloud contains flourishing, cuddly sex, warm fuzzies, "childlike" wonder, etc. The overlap contains such values as thrills, security, unconditional self-love, curiosity and humor.

It's not that all these values are bad per se, so much as they are undeveloped or misdirected: The primalist is taking an incredible amount for granted by not challenging his values. Furthermore, a given value might mean something different in the mind of a primalist from what it does in the mind of a rational adult. "Security" for an animal primalist means eliminating threats. For a child primalist it means "someone to take care of me." And for a rational adult it means "planning for the future." All of the values mentioned above are spun in various ways by various primalists and reason-oriented people and cannot be taken at face value.

Let's look at two shared values in detail. Curiosity is a value for almost all primalists. However, we're not talking about the curiosity of a Richard Feynman, but a form of curiosity that is rather like Attention Deficit Disorder. It's scattered, pulled this way and that by top-ten lists, "amazing" science stories, celebrity gossip, details about serial murder, wanting to know what's under that bikini, and quizzes about what type of vegetable you are. This "idle curiosity," as it used to be called, is trained into children by *Sesame Street*, which bombards youngsters with information and shifting frames of reference. This distracting style is greatly encouraged by use of the Internet, which has to be used with great discipline (i.e. reason) if it is not to encourage ADD-like habits of mind. The tragedy here is that many primalists, especially child ones, kid themselves that they are curious like Richard Feynman when they are really just Pretenders, treating knowledge as entertainment, rather than as something that requires you to change your life. Scattered curiosity fits in well with the deep passivity that comes from not deriving one's values from reason: In both cases the ship drifts unsteered.

The Splendor of the Soul

Another value that can have several meanings is wonder. I want to linger over this value, because it is a key concept of this book, since a mature wonder lies close to the center of a healthy soul.

Let me first say that mature wonder, as the name implies, is a relatively late addition to our mental toolkit. We start, of course, with childlike wonder, which is the reaction that toddlers and even grown-ups have to soap bubbles, tile floors and fairy tales. This kind of wonder is spontaneous and ingenuous and is a blessing upon existence. But it is not enough to get one through life beyond childhood.

As we become adults, we tend to feel this kind of wonder less often. We have seen soap bubbles a hundred times, and we develop a network of superficial, "practical" concepts that we snap everything up in as we try to get through our daily routines. Everything is seen in terms of its everyday use: A tile floor becomes just something to stand on. Furthermore, fairy tales do not really speak to our adult concerns. We are in danger of going through lives in a kind of pragmatic trance. The remedy for this is what I call mature wonder.

Mature wonder isn't a natural feeling one has at something unexpected and amazing. It is, rather, a choice: We choose to see the world in a certain way, and simultaneously, we choose to be a certain some-thing: We choose to see what we are regarding afresh, as if we've never seen it before. And we choose to be someone who lives more than a banal existence, who lets life touch us, instead of living in a cocoon of quotidian routines.

The wonder of a child, although it can through many repetitions shape his sense of life, is essentially ephemeral: It lasts the moment and is gone. But mature wonder is something you incorporate into your soul as a permanent attitude. I remember Rainer Maria Rilke's justly famous poem, "Archaic Torso of Apollo," about a headless statue from ancient times. The poem describes how the beauty of the statue's missing eyes shines through its various remaining parts like a dimmed lamp. It continues by saying that there's no part of its body that does not see you. Then it abruptly concludes: You must change your life.

That is the meaning of mature wonder: You must change your life. You must see the world for what it is and become who you are. This sounds onerous, but really it's beautiful. To take a modest example: I gaze upon the vertical blinds behind my desk. I wonder at their length and graceful curvature, and I delight in the pattern of shading on the curves. I am amazed that someone created a machine to make them. And I love the way they break the view of the woods outside into stripes of cream and green.

This is no trivial experience. Things as ordinary as vertical blinds change my life because seeing them as I do forbids me to see reality as ordinary. If I can't take even the blinds for granted, then I can't take nature for granted, or man's works, or my wife, or myself. If I let the experience of mature wonder really permeate me, then it becomes impossible for me to see the world as some people do, as one big office cubicle and myself as a drone.

Mature wonder involves an appreciation of beauty, but it is not mere aestheticism. The world is not my bauble and I am no mere connoisseur of beautiful objects. The world is real to me, and as a living human being, I am far more than a mere spectator of it. The engine that powers mature wonder is not a view of the world as eye candy, but life, which demands that I act in the real world and that I realize my potential.

For the primalist, wonder is usually a different matter. Animal primalists don't usually feel much wonder, because they're too concerned with being tough, although some of them are secret sentimentalists. (Some of them feel a kind of wonder-like awe at big, powerful or even scary things.) Child primalists, however, would count wonder as one of their core values. Many child primalists pride themselves on their sense of wonder and believe it to be authentically childlike, and of course, sometimes it is. But as often as not it is only "childlike" wonder, a mere simulation of the real thing. The problem is that they are trying to recreate the wonder that a child feels, a kind of wonder that spontaneously bowls one over and leaves one's mouth hanging open. They usually aren't willing to go to the trouble of looking for wonder in real things, like the design of an apartment building or the conscience of an Oskar Schindler. They tend to need special effects— magic and spaceships—to glorify existence. What's worse, as Pretenders, they tend to look at objects of wonder as entertainment. They cheapen things by calling them "cool," or worse: "awesome." (There's no word that more sucks the awe out of things than "awesome" as it is currently used.) They act like perpetual 13-year-olds.

Today's culture encourages people to be adolescent in their tastes and manners forever, eternal foulmouthed "rebels" who never grow out of their teenage, or even tweenage, taste in movies, music and books. When this includes aggressiveness and predatory sexuality, it is animal primalism. Build in a love of quirkiness and "childlike" wonder, and you get child primalism. Either way, reason, judgment, decorum and taste are out of the picture.

This essay, which is the first of two parts, tackles the development of the primalist types in the twentieth century, while the sequel shows how primalism has evolved through its interaction with modern technology to yield the salient personality type of the early twenty-first. I want to start out by giving brief "classic" examples of animal and child primalism from the 1960s. Next we'll consider some of the primalist's characteristic ways of thought. Then we'll discuss how primalism came about. After that we'll look at full-length portraits of primalists closer to our own day, and we'll conclude with a discussion of the linkage between reason and values, a linkage which, if properly understood, would nip primalism in the bud.

Animal Magnetism and Childish Charm

When you look for the animal version of primalism, what you should look for are characteristics like machismo, earthiness, lustiness or strong will, not animality in the sense of eating with your snout in your food. A good example would be John F. Kennedy. President Kennedy was a quintessentially "manly" man. He valued promiscuous sex, and he pursued the most over-feminized woman of her time, Marilyn Monroe. He sought power and status. He was reckless (i.e. craved thrills). He associated with the Rat Pack (a group of entertainers that used an animal name to symbolize their Cool nature). His social structure was based more on his first family than his second, and he felt toward his father and brothers a Mafia-like loyalty. He looked upon the battle with communism as a macho contest (who had the most missiles, etc.). His popularity came from a visceral source, charisma.

JFK was the alpha male of America. Kennedy's success suggests that some form of animal primalism was popular in his day. This is not to say that Kennedy howled at the moon. He could be quite rational on some subjects, strategic and composed. A person who was a pure animal primalist would be a brute or a bitter cynic. But even though Kennedy did have table manners, he was quite different from a leader such as Abraham Lincoln who had no surface charisma and who was elected president on the basis of his powers of rational and moral persuasion, as evinced in the Lincoln-Douglas debates and the Cooper Union speech. The premier medium of Lincoln's day, the newspaper, played up Lincoln's attractive qualities, while the premier medium of Kennedy's day, television, played up Kennedy's. We will return to the connection between the media and primalism in the next essay.

If you want to get some idea of what a general

animal primalist is like, look at the concepts he uses. Table 1 shows some of the slogans and sayings of the typical animal primalist.

[Table 1] Assorted Concepts and Catch Phrases of Animal Primalism

- Survival of the fittest
- He who has the most toys when he dies, wins
- Mano a mano
- Work hard, play hard
- Respect (for me) and loyalty (to me)
- Sexual conquests
- "Man up"
- Nature red in tooth and claw

Turning to the child variant of primalism, you might look for characteristics such as "innocence" or "openness," which I deliberately put in scare-quotes. Our classic example of child primalism would be the hippies. The hippies believed in playfulness and cuddliness. They believed in being ingenuously "natural" in their hygiene, hairstyle, food and sex. The hippies were sensual in a "childlike" way and craved wondrous new experiences, including those gained with LSD. They chanted, sang, and picketed about Love, Love, Love—unconditional "love" of everybody for everybody, sexual "love" for strangers, "love" for the sun, the moon and the stars. The hippie's native habitat was the commune, which is based on the value of "sharing," a precept designed for children.

When hippies attempted their rebellious humor they believed they were speaking truth to power like the little child in "The Emperor's New Clothes," but usually they were just being adolescent smart-asses. (For example, the behavior in court of the Chicago Seven.) Child primalists are not alone in their belief that they can blow through the bullshit with humor. Animal primalists, when they're not trying to dominate someone with their wit, also fancy that they are exposing other people's hypocrisies with their jokes and jibes.

Primalism of both kinds encourages this kind of behavior because it fosters the belief that since we all have the same, preset values, we all know the same truths. If someone doesn't acknowledge those truths, then he is either lying or self-deluded and either way it is fair to use sarcasm to bring the truth out into the open. Likewise, when the hippies staged their mass demonstrations and took buildings and college administrators hostage, they thought they were exercising some kind of liberating "soul force" on the order of King or Gandhi, but really they were just employing the force of numbers to disrupt the lives of innocent bystanders. One really has to believe in one's childlike innocence to be that self-righteous.

I'm not a cynic when it comes to child primalists. Many of them are quite charming. But an adult who tries to live with a child's values is not going to be childlike in a natural and innocent way. Rather she is going to be a *distortion* of a child. We are talking about people who were in one or more important ways very immature, *immature on principle*. And they would brag about this.

Table 2 shows some slogans and bumper stickers associated with child primalism.

[Table 2] Assorted Concepts and Catch Phrases of Child Primalism

- Childlike wonder
- Free hugs
- Imagine/Believe/Hope/Change
- May the Force be with you
- Work as play
- Make love, not war
- The Darwin fish with legs
- Mother Nature

The varieties of primalism are parts of clouds, not monoliths. They are messy human artifacts, clusters of characteristics that are have a certain adhesiveness to them, but that are definitely not carved in stone. I don't want the reader to lock in on a single example of each variant. Ernest Hemingway, Madonna or any random hardcore rapper could serve as examples of an animal primalist just as easily as Kennedy. (For a fictional example, you can't top Frank Underwood from *House of Cards*.) For the child variant I could have used Marilyn Monroe, Wes Anderson or a random member of the Occupy Movement rather than the hippies. (Almost any regular character from *Star Trek: The Next Generation* would serve as a good fictional example.) A primalist who is a bit of both might be Howard Stern, with his almost childlike smuttiness, or various "slackers." Please keep in mind that the categories of primalists are not "natural kinds" like chemical elements: People don't sign up for primalist clubs, they aren't pure, and they don't wear labels.

Be that as it may, if you look around you, you will see how common these ways of looking at values are. Quite a few businesspeople believe in animal-value primalism. Few actually steal, but a number skirt the law on a regular basis and many believe in ruthless competition, ruthless treatment of employees, etc. Quite a few people on the political left believe in child-value primalism. Liberals do not typically go around hugging everyone, but they do hold the "childlike" fantasy that money can be spent without being earned. Many people who are fanatics about spectator sports or violent action movies and TV shows are animal primalists. Many people who practice child-centered parenting or who like folk music are child primalists. The two types converge on liking comic book movies, which is probably why they are so popular.

You can distinguish the types of primalists by their attitudes. Animal primalists tend to be cynics or "realists." They believe that conflict is inevitable and that organizations run on personal loyalty, for the benefit of those in the organization, especially those at the top. Child primalists tend to be naïve or "idealists." They believe that cooperation is natural and that organizations should run on self-actualization for the benefit of all employees, customers and society. Animal primalists are more often men than women, but there are plenty of lusty women who could serve as counter-examples. (Think of the "cougar" type.) Child primalists in my experience are about evenly split between men and women. Animal primalists usually overstress the differences between males and females, and child primalists usually understress them. I have no way of knowing how many people are primalists to some degree, but they can be seen at all levels of American society.

I hope you now have some idea of what a primalist is like. For our portraits of the two types to be meaningful, however, we need to contrast them with the type of person who derives his values from reason. A good classic example of the principled individual might be Neil Armstrong, the first human being on the moon. Armstrong was a patient, modest, careful man, who excelled as a pilot and an astronaut not because of any macho stunts, but because of his calm attention to detail. He was an Eagle Scout in his youth and a deist as an adult, which suggest that he was serious about principles. He refused glory after his moon landing and sought a teaching position. He was no philosopher, but his actions demonstrated that he believed values come from reason and not directly from our animal or child nature, although he might not have used those words to describe himself.

Although they don't think in bumper stickers as much as primalists do, people who base their values on reason have their catch phrases also.

[Table 3] Assorted Concepts and Catch Phrases of Principled People

- Be reasonable
- Look at the big picture
- Put yourself in the other guy's shoes
- Respect others/Respect yourself
- Commitment (in romantic love)
- Work as craftsmanship
- Liberty and justice for all
- Lawful nature

Once upon a time it was normal for Americans to live by rational principles and maxims, such as "Honesty is the best policy." Even religious precepts in America were to some extent colored by rational values in the wake of the Enlightenment. Now the role of reason in many people's lives is not to help them figure out the kind of life they ought to lead but to help them obtain the things they unreflectively desire. Most Americans are essentially consumers, and fairly indiscriminant ones at that, rather than being primarily producers of their own values and connoisseurs of values produced by others.

I looked at the 50 titles that were most commonly shelved as "self-help" by Goodreads members. Books that offer advice for life rarely talk about fundamental values, but instead counsel us on technique (*The 7 Habits of Highly Effective People*) or strive to help people clarify and attain primalist values (*Men are from Mars, Women are from Venus.*). Only one—a Christian book called *The Purpose-Driven Life*, by Rick Warren— actually seemed to deal with the big questions. The idea that fundamental values need to be discovered, chosen, and realized rationally, while not extinct in America today, is certainly not the norm.

I hope the reader doesn't get the impression that primalism is just a matter of personal style and that primalists are merely interesting characters, just amiable rascals and loveable geeks. While that is true much of the time (allowing for the use of the word "geek," which I do not approve of), primalists have a dark side, too. Animal primalists can be ruthless is their exploitation of others, up to and including rape, while child primalists, when they're not blocking the streets, represent a kind of winsome debasement of the intellect, because they often have no real passion and have trouble getting anything done. These syndromes deserve to be taken seriously.

The Three Faces of Primalism

Primalists, like everyone else, have many mental tools in their toolboxes, and different primalists use them in different ways. In this section of the essay I will describe three such tools, implicit techniques of framing and experiencing the self that are part of how primalism functions. I will be focusing on the bad aspects of these tools, but one should keep in mind that they do have some good aspects, too.

The first of these tools I call the proxy self. The proxy self is your game face, the avatar you send in to represent you in a situation that you believe to be a contest, battle or drama. Examples of the proxy self in-

clude the postures that people assume during tough negotiations and the aloof front that some men put on in their quest for respect. People who believe that life-is a zero-sum game tend to use a proxy self to go out and fight their battles. Poker, the classic zero-sum game, involves a proxy self, because you bluff and try to send false tells to the other players.

Using a proxy self is not always bad; for example, it is legitimate in diplomacy, in customer service or in dealing with seriously irrational people. Unfortunately, however, some animal primalists, because they think human life is a fight to get what you want, adopt the proxy self to manipulate colleagues or to get someone into bed. The child primalist, on the other hand, sometimes uses the proxy self in a sneaky or passive-aggressive way to get what she wants from someone she views as a power-figure. Pouting, for example, is often a way of putting on a proxy self. This, of course, reflects the child's view of frustration: She doesn't get what she desires because someone with more power denies it to her, and since she thinks of herself as helpless, she feels it's OK to manipulate that person to get what she wants. Note that both animal and child primalists believe that life is a power struggle. Consequently, neither deals with other people as equals.

A Circle of Souls

The second tool is the group mind. This tool involves the synchronization of mental functioning so that people in the same circle share the same pseudo sense of life, running jokes, rationalistic ideas, etc.

People in group-mind mode can ping off of each other effortlessly, even to the point of finishing one another's sentences. The mirror neurons are working overtime here. The group mind is a kind of shared trance and can seem almost like telepathy.

The group mind can be found wherever values are shared, including rational ones, but it is most frequently used to bond people who share non-philosophical traits such as gender, family, race, membership in a college fraternity, an affinity for comic books, etc. This kind of bonding becomes problematic when members of the group expect loyalty based on group membership rather than on shared principles. When a group mind is based on family, ethnicity or hierarchical loyalty, it is usually a function of animal primalism. When a group mind is based on membership in the human race or on real or imagined sympathy, then it is typically child primalism that is at work.

Religion is often a foundation for the group mind, and congregations over the millenia often form a group mind based on singing, clapping and the "presence of the Holy Spirit." More recently, Elvis Presley was practically a new Jesus to his fans, and the Beatles were bigger than Jesus, as John Lennon said. They inaugurated a new pagan religion, one that was at first based on music and dance and then later on casual sex and drugs. Some of the liturgical services this new religion has celebrated have been so intense that people have literally danced themselves to death. The adherents of this religion can be animal primalists (for example, some fans of the Rolling Stones or rap) or child primalists (such as some fans of the early Beatles or twee), with other people straddling the line. Please note once again that one cannot use a single trait such as liking the Rolling Stones as an infallible sign of primalism: It is just one tile in the mosaic.

The group mind is legitimate in activities such as team sports, ensemble music performance and love-making, but it is positively dangerous in others. You don't want to invest in a stock just because everybody else is investing in it, and if you're a girl, you really don't want to join the bacchanalia at a fraternity party. Most of our daily operations require individual judgment. Sure, it's OK to be part of a cheering crowd of 10,000 fans at the occasional basketball game, but you can't spend your life that way. The problem is that a lot of people *do* want to spend a significant portion of their lives this way. Extreme animal primalists want to form packs, carried along by sexual frenzy, fanatic enthusiasm or even aggression. This can lead to gay-bashing and gang rape. Some child primalists want everyone to join the love-in and "occupy" public areas, often living like teenagers who never clean up after themselves.

I suppose I must sound a bit like John Adams, with his fear of the mob. I do fear the mob within each of us, but I don't think that the group mind necessarily results in mob behavior. Non-individuated states of mind play an important role in the economy of the soul. But it's important to remember that while the group mind has its place, it becomes destructive if it dislodges crisp, focused reason as our baseline mental state. An individuated state is not just a tool one turns on at 9 a.m. and turns off at 5 p.m. The focused self, the rational self, should be the craftsman who uses the tools.

The Third-Person Perspective

The last mental tool we will look at in this essay is the third-person perspective on the self. This occurs when someone views a part of himself as "it" instead of "I." If one feels controlled by forces outside one's rational consciousness, such as preset values, then those forces will likely seem foreign to one's self and will be experienced in the third person instead of the first. Consider as an example the way in which some religious people are tormented by their sexual desires, which seem to bubble up from the demonic region that is the body. Many people end up viewing some of their values and mental functions paradoxically, as both self and non-self. You see this perspective in people who objectify themselves and say "Well, that's just the kind of person I am" or "That's my _____ expressing itself," where the blank is filled by "inner child" or "reptilian brain" or "id."

"Id" is a telling example. The term is from Freud's theory of psychoanalysis and means the unconscious part of the psyche where instinctive impulses originate. Freud's German term, "Es," just means "it," but for some reason Freud's translators thought it best to use the Latin word for "it" instead of the English word. In any case, Freud clearly meant for us to regard a part of ourselves literally in the third person.

Interestingly, an attempt has been made by psychoanalyst Roy Schafer to purge Freud's thinking of the third-person perspective. In his book *A New Language for Psychoanalysis,* Schafer states that what is needed are statements in which *I* do something rather than ones in which some construct does it. This idea can be profitably transferred to other schools of psychology that fall into the trap of a third-person perspective, while leaving behind the baggage of Freud's arcane and arbitrary system.

People who adopt a third-person perspective have a tendency to separate themselves from their emotions and personal characteristics. Either they will make themselves into a character in a narrative, saying things like "I'm a survivor," or they will they will Pretend emotions that they believe they are "supposed" to feel, as in, for example, acting tough because "boys don't cry." Life for such people becomes theater and they create a proxy self, not to manipulate others but to manage themselves. This is a kind of Pretederism.

Animal primalists commonly adopt a third-person perspective as they look at the biological factors that they think influence behavior. They might explain the way they overreacted to something as a "fight or flight" response. Child primalists sometimes focus, not surprisingly, on childhood trauma and other forms of victimhood. I don't want to discount all these explanations. Some experiences really are so extreme that they cause a "rupture" between conscious and unconscious functioning so that some force that doesn't seem like the self might temporarily control one. However, it is my sense that many primalists resort to such explanations much too casually, in a kind of psychological hypochondria motivated by misguided philosophy. Sadly, these diagnoses are often little more than ways to avoid taking responsibility for one's actions.

Some aspects of the self really should be viewed in something like the third person, but many should not. We really do have a "reptilian" brain, although that does not mean that it functions independently of the rest of the person. However, we do not have a super-ego, id or unconscious in Freud's sense. None of this has stopped millions of victims of bad psychology from analyzing themselves in third-person terms and becoming self-alienated. The third-person perspective is part of the process by which half-digested science trickles down to form part of everyday fantasies. Modern biology, psychology and to some extent economics provide many opportunities to regard oneself in the third person.

Many people who take a scientific view of human beings do not believe in free will and thus attribute their actions to causes outside of consciousness. Because of this determinists are forced into a third-person perspective. Despite this, some philosophers have attempted arabesques of fancy footwork to try to dance their way out of it (e.g. the philosophical contradiction in terms known as compatibilism, which is the notion that we are both determined and free).

However, not all primalists deny the existence of free will. Many animal primalists believe in the importance of the force of will because they think life is a struggle and that willpower plays a key role. Child primalists, as far as I have observed, rarely believe in determinism, as they almost universally believe that we can choose love, kindness, peace, etc. Most primalists of both kinds seem to believe that one has a limited but real range of free choices: They believe one can follow one's true nature or to deny it, but they don't think there are any alternatives to our preset values, except for perversion or weakness. If you don't follow your alleged nature, an animal primalist will say that you're not a "real man" or "real woman," and a child primalist will say that you're "sick" or "twisted." This isn't a very robust notion of free will, but it isn't determinism. A person who believes that values are developed by reason recognizes that many value-systems are possible to adult human beings. Even though most of them are wrong, they are not necessarily perversions, just mistakes usually based on limited knowledge.

Where Did Primalism Come From?

Primalism has a complicated family tree. I'm going to sketch out a few of the branches, but please keep in mind that this is a simplification. To tell the entire story would require a whole book.

Modern primalism grew out of science and philosophy, but it has precursors in attitudes that people have held since time immemorial. In the case of animal primalism, the primary forerunner is old-fashioned, non-intellectual cynicism. Cynicism tells us that everybody is really looking out for #1 and that all that people really want are food, sex, ego satisfactions and the like. The cynic seems to believe, in a pre-Darwinian, way that people are just animals. The cynic feels that it is appropriate to use a deceptive proxy self to get what he wants because "nice guys finish last." Cynics tend to think that non-cynics are fools, weak, self-deluded or are perhaps just running a subtler con. You can see old-fashioned cynicism (verging on nihilism) in *Reservoir Dogs*.

If cynicism is the precursor to animal primalism, then the Romantic celebration of innocence and wonder is the precursor to the child variant. The idealization of the child goes back at least to Rousseau and Wordsworth, and modern liberal Christianity celebrates the openness and splendor of the child in its own way as well. These attitudes are taken for granted in American culture, except among child-hating religious fanatics.

Cynicism acquired a "scientific" pedigree after Darwin's theories came to be understood and misunderstood in the late nineteenth century. The view that males are just well-dressed cave men and that females are just breeders fueled the development of college football, professionalized boxing, big game hunting and other "manly" pursuits—basically, the Teddy Roosevelt ideal of masculinity. Then, at the turn of the twentieth century came Freudian psychoanalysis and its theory of instincts, which served to convince generations of intellectuals and lay people that human behavior was entirely motivated by sex, jealousy and aggressiveness. The Freudians argued that healthy adjustment requires that one repress or "sublimate" one's infantile, animalistic, savage urges, which we never grow out of and which lie seething beneath the surface our whole lives.

The amount of suffering these views have caused is incalculable. Thousands if not tens of thousands of men have been rendered permanently punch drunk by repeated concussions in the ring and on the gridiron. Millions of women have believed that that they should not have careers and that they were not going to be fulfilled unless they had first, the approved kind of orgasm and then a baby.

This "brutes in suits" view of human nature, as John

Pettegrew calls it, declined to some extent after WWI, partly because the senseless carnage of trench warfare convinced many that contemporary views of manhood were just a fraud, and partly because thinkers like anthropologist Margaret Mead convinced many people that with the right "nurture" people were capable of a kind and non-jealous way of life with a free sexuality—meaning that people did not have preset, violent values, as Freud and the Darwinists claimed. Mead's emphasis on "nurture" over "nature" dovetailed nicely with the Marxism of America's "Red Decade," which held that human personality is infinitely malleable. All this helps explain the improbable alliance of Mead's ideas, communism and bohemianism in America, since all three views were more or less utopian and promised to remove aggression from human affairs. But Freudianism, along with an even more reductionistic school of psychology of the early twentieth century, behaviorism, hung on.

Starting in the 1940s, psychologists such as Abraham Maslow and Carl Rogers tried to counter psychoanalysis and behaviorism with what came to be known as "Third Force," or humanistic, psychology. These views did not couch human nature in terms of instincts per se, as animal primalism did, but in terms of needs and tendencies, which were more or less universal and which would (in Maslow's version, at least) be addressed in a hierarchy: bodily needs first, social needs next, and spiritual needs last. The humanistic psychologists did not emphasize competition, aggressiveness and dragging women off by their hair as the animal primalists did—their concerns were softer and had more to do with being accepted by others and with self-actualization through creativity—but they still spoke in terms of innate needs, drives or desires.

It would not be fair to blame modern child primalism entirely on humanistic psychology, which is far more sophisticated than primalism is, but one does feed the other. Child primalism seems, in large part, to be a bastardization and oversimplification of the views of Maslow and Mead, as well as, among others, Benjamin Spock, (the popular postwar baby doctor) and later, Eric Berne, whose I'm OK, You're OK school of Transactional Analysis extolled the emotional primacy of the Child ego state. This theoretical scion of humanistic psychology was grafted onto the rootstock of America's tendency to idolize the child.

The humanists must shoulder some of the blame for the direction this bastardization took, because of their emphasis on preset values rather than principled reason as the foundation of action. In reality, only animals and very young children are dominated by preset values, and since the humanistic psychologists were too, well, humane to make man out to be a beast, by implication they suggested that man is a child. Their views were simplified into full-blown child primalism as they filtered through the culture. However, I don't think most child primalists explicitly lean on Wordsworth and Maslow in the same explicit way many animal primalists have leaned on Darwin and Freud. Ideas about the innocent, curious, loving nature of children seem to be floating anonymously in American culture, ready to be tapped into. It's worth keeping in mind that people can have a psychologically vested interest in feeling innocent and vulnerable just as much as they can about feeling powerful and aggressive.

The New Left and feminism in the 1960s and 1970s embraced the child primalism engendered by the Third Force psychologists, but added their own bizarre mixture of adulterated Freud and Marx. They discounted Freud's warning about the dangers of unchecked instincts and said that if only capitalism would stop repressing us, we would all be loving, sexually ecstatic, childlike beings. Pieces of this strange synthesis can be found in a mild form in Erich Fromm and more floridly in Herbert Marcuse.

The American left in the 1960s and beyond wanted to believe, à *la* Rousseau, that if only the corrupting influences of society were reformed, people would be naturally good. This put the left in conflict with their own Marxism, a school of thought that is strictly deterministic and that believes the developments of history to be the product of inevitable class conflicts that will be resolved only by violence. Ironically, most sixties radicals and their successors believed so much in morality and innate moral goodness that they simply couldn't maintain a consistent determinist or a pro-violence outlook—like good Americans, they thought we could improve society by good intentions and a little "soul force," a notion antithetical to Marxism. That is why American radicals were rarely as bloody as their German or Italian counterparts, who were trying to precipitate literal class warfare because they believed the bourgeois were beyond persuasion. Child primalism, as false as it is, probably saved many American lives in that era.

Primalism, mostly of the child variety, is also responsible for the near-obliteration of at least one of the most important rational value-concepts: self-esteem. The concept of self-esteem attracted attention as an important value when Ayn Rand and her student Nathaniel Branden developed it in the 1960s. To them it meant the self-respect that one earns by being the best person one can be. But in the hands of the child primalists, self-esteem came to mean unconditional self-love. Jean M. Twenge and W. Keith Campbell document the effects of this distortion of self-esteem in their book *The Narcissism Epidemic*. They relate how parents dress their little kids up in T-shirts that say "Princess" and "Rock Star," and how kindergarten teachers teach them to sing, "I am special, I am special, Look at me, Look at me," to the tune of "Frère Jacques." Unconditional self-love, which in its extreme forms becomes narcissism, is a primal value in both animal and child primalism and has led to generations of American young people feeling a powerful sense of entitlement and a near-pathological desire for attention, the latest manifestation of which would be the reality TV show *Bridezilla*.

The child primalism of the 1960s has had an enormous influence in politics, education and culture, but intellectually it has been largely displaced by a theory that came to be known as evolutionary psychology. The founding documents of this school of thought were E. O. Wilson's *Sociobiology* and Richard Dawkins' *The Selfish Gene*. It holds that human desires and behavior are determined by the survival and reproductive advantages they conferred on our ancestors.

There is a new and paradoxical take on the proxy self in evolutionary psychology. According to the traditional primalist view, the conscious self sends the proxy self out to fight its battles. According to the views of evolutionary psychology, consciousness *is* a proxy self, sent out by our genes to fight *their* battles. As Dawkins states, we are all just robots operated by our genes. This is the third-person perspective with a vengeance, and in the wake of this development, alienation from the self has become almost complete for some people. Some of evolutionary psychology's philosophical allies hold that there is no such thing as the self at all, which means that we are pure "it" with no "I." Under this banner, animal primalism has triumphed among a considerable number of educated Americans, who view it as nearly self-evident.

Evolutionary psychology clearly has some merits, but it is often more speculative than empirical. Its primary argumentative gambit is to invent semi-plausible, ad hoc accounts of how a certain behavior furthered the biological interests of our ancestors, and then to say that that justifies or explains current behavior. These "just-so" stories are often little more than rationalizations for how some people happen to feel and act. The result in some quarters is a deep and amoral cynicism. Theorists Craig Palmer and Randy Thornhill have gone so far as to say that rape is, biologically speaking, a good strategy for a certain type of male. Of course, they would say that rape is morally wrong, but since morality according to this view is only just another biological excretion, their demurral doesn't carry much weight. Determinism is the norm among evolutionary psychologists, but the non-intellectual primalists who borrow their ideas do not seem usually to adopt this tenet of the theory, because they are concerned with strength and force of will.

I don't want to leave the reader with the idea that I

am anti-science. I believe in evolution, genes and adaptation, and Darwin is one of my heroes, but at the same time I believe that evolutionary psychology, despite some of its useful insights, has seriously overstepped its bounds and is a potential disaster in terms of its effects on human well being. Much of it is not science, but *scientism*, the intellectually corrupt misuse of science. I don't want to derail the discussion of primalism with an extended refutation of the worst aspects of evolutionary psychology, so I'll just refer the reader to Raymond Tallis' book *Aping Mankind: Neuromania, Darwinitis and the Misrepresentation of Humanity* and to my pamphlet *Free Will: A Response to Sam Harris*, available on Kindle.

To sum up: animal primalism is in the intellectual ascendancy because of its associations with hard science, while child primalism lingers as a cultural force, because it appeals to idealistic and humanistic impulses as well as to left-wing dreams of remaking human personality. Both forms of primalism have trickled down to the general public by means of social science and self-help books. Relying on oversimplified science and worshipping the idols of the media, the public jumps to intellectual and emotional conclusions and holds primalist ideas largely in the form of pseudo sense of life, playing out fantasies of sex and power or hugs and wonder, as the case may be.

Enter Philosophy, Making Matters Worse

There is one major non-scientific stream that feeds primalism in modern America. It is not a theory of needs or hungers as such, but a school of philosophy that deals with the nature and scope of knowledge, the distinctively American school: pragmatism. According to major pragmatist philosophers William James (1843-1910) and John Dewey (1859-1952), truth is not a matter of ideas corresponding to facts but of thought processes that get us what we want. As James said, "the 'true' is only the expedient in our way of thinking, just as the 'right' is only the expedient in our way of behaving." This is usually summarized as "truth is what works." Dewey shows us the political implications of this kind of thinking when he adds, "Legislation is a matter of more or less intelligent improvisation aiming at palliating conditions by means of patchwork policies."

It should be obvious from ideas like these that such a philosophy takes for granted what people happen to desire rather than urging them to establish consistent principles. A practicing pragmatist would tend to be more concerned with taking care of immediate, concrete, unexamined needs, such as those that primalism posits. Pragmatism has had an enormous influence on American life through Dewey's theories of progressive education and Franklin Roosevelt's experimental attitude toward governance during the New Deal, when desperation weakened a panicked populace's attachment to principles. There is a strong current in American thought that says that whatever works is OK—whatever works to help the nation, whatever works to help the poor, whatever works to help the individual realize his fantasies. We don't need principles, we don't need a fixed Constitution, we don't need reality—we don't even need grammar. All we need is "more or less intelligent improvisation" as we surf over waves of innate desires that well up from within us. Pragmatism so perfectly reinforces the primalism of biology and psychology that the reader would be forgiven for wondering whether there was a conspiracy to assassinate reason. Together, all of these factors work to bring about what C. S. Lewis called, in another context, The Abolition of Man.

Just One of the Guys

At the beginning of this essay, we looked at John Kennedy and the hippies as specific examples of primalists from the 1960s. Now I would like to share more general and up-to-date portraits of animal and child primalists, as well as a picture of a person of reason. Although primalists are not all alike, these examples are a bit more representative of contemporary types and could easily be people the reader might know.

A modern fish swims at the confluence of cynicism, scientism and sexual game playing. I call him "the Guy." The Guy is an animal primalist. He is usually male, although there are a lot more female Guys than there used to be. The Guy is the epitome of a Fast-Time Pretender. He Pretends a casual, earthy, cynical, knowing sense of life, based on role models from the media and his buddies. He takes for granted that women are to be used. He likes nothing so much as sports, action movies, porn, and other junk food; and he pees on the seat in public bathrooms. Like other men with an enthusiastic proxy self, the Guy loves to bullshit. This immature type is found at all socioeconomic levels, from working-class bars to college dorms to corporate boardrooms. A lot of the younger ones seem unable to grow out of zombie stories and video games and to leave home and find a wife and a career. This failure-to-launch male became a problem even before the recent economic downturn.

If and when the Guy does get a job and a girl, she treats him with affectionate patronization. This is due to many women having backed away from egalitarian feminism to what I call "gender primalism," which holds that men are essentially a certain way, needing such things as sports and a man cave, while women are another way, needing shoes and babies. Gender primalism advocates accepting these facts, benevolently humoring the opposite sex and even oneself. This humoring of the opposite sex is a mild form of the proxy self. The humoring of oneself is the third-person perspective. (Listen to the amused way many women talk about their "boobs" as almost not a part of themselves.) The Bible of gender primalism is John Gray's bestseller, *Men are from Mars, Women are from Venus.*

The difference between the Guy and the traditional cynic lies in his reliance on modern scientific "knowledge" about human nature and the sexes. Science (i.e. scientism) justifies the Guy's indulgence in low tastes and keeps him from exploring anything higher. But the Guy doesn't buy into the worldview of scientism completely. He doesn't believe that he is a robot operated by his genes. He believes himself to be a lion or a wolf or in extreme cases a pig and that it is appropriate in the struggle for existence to use a proxy self to get what he naturally wants. Life demands that you act tough and "go for it." As befits a sub-rational way of thinking, the Guy's rhetoric is visceral and crudely direct. (The earthiness of the animal primalist and the rebelliousness of the 1960s child primalist have conspired to drag American English down to a scatological level. We now think that by being foul-mouthed, we're being frank and natural.)

The Guy operates on a duality. He and his male friends typically feel great loyalty to each other, like a bunch of dogs sleeping in a heap. They share the same cynical values and usually form a group mind as they hang out together, playing video games and getting wasted. They sometimes stage little insult contests and play practical jokes on each other, but they generally operate on a consensus based on a common pseudo sense of life and a shared Bubble Universe, punctuated by pouting and mild acts of violence, such as fighting over the remote.

The other half of the duality is the Guy's attitude toward women, which can verge on the predatory. He tells his girl he loves her (proxy self speaking), and a little part of him means it, but he also thinks he is justified in saying it even when he doesn't mean it all that much, in order to get into her pants (ruthless biological self thinking). This can get quite slimy, because the Law of the Jungle doesn't leave much room for empathy. And since heartfelt and thoughtful encounters with reality and other people are what tutor desire into full maturity, the Guy will inevitably be emotionally stunted, unless and until he chooses to give up being a Guy and starts becoming a man. Guys who grow up and do something with their lives, but remain animal primalists are likely to be conservative when it comes to electoral politics and a shark when it comes to corporate politics, believing in the survival of the fittest and using other people on their way up the ladder.

I should say that while the Guy can sometimes be unappetizing, he can also be a benevolent father, because he understands kids, being one himself. In addition, Guys are often the first people through the door in an emergency. Like most human types, they have their strengths as well as their weaknesses. Their responsibility for what they have become is somewhat mitigated by the fact that they are in over their heads intellectually. Trying to shame a Guy into changing, as many feminists have attempted to do, is not very productive. What is needed is a defense of reason in values so that men do not feel justified in acting like animals. Feminism, with its own anti-reason tendencies, is not going to be of much help here.

Animal primalism, in conjunction with the implosion of serious art and philosophy in the twentieth century, has contributed to a general dumbing down of men and women's concerns during the last 100 years. Many intelligent people chase primal values such as casual sex, electronic toys, and sensationalistic entertainment, because they think that primal things are what people really *should* want, since that is our nature. Our modern worship of the primitive, the proletarian and the puerile is born of this fortified cynicism. Add into the mix the inferiority many middle-class folk feel toward black people, cool people and celebrities because of their alleged greater vitality and virility, and what you get is a triangle of steel that blocks cultural progress. And here we squat.

Attack of the Warm Fuzzies

I call our representative child primalist Chris, an androgynous name for an androgynous person. Chris can be spotted by his casual, non-threatening appearance. Where the Guy typically wears a T-shirt with a sports team name on it, Chris wears one with a joke about pi on it. Glasses are common. She-Chris sometimes wears more gender-marked clothes than He-Chris, but when she does there is often something old-fashioned about her long dresses and long hair.

Chris is a computer programmer and longs to work at the Googleplex for an employer who understands that creativity and play go together. Chris will never get to the Googleplex, however, because he keeps getting fired for going to staff meetings and pointing out how his boss screwed up something, instead of taking his boss aside and discussing the problem in an impersonal way. Chris has values that seems very obvious to her and cannot understand how others don't think the same way. She has a bumper sticker that says, "What If They Held a War and Nobody Came?" The Guy loves to laugh at Chris, especially at He-Chris, whom he regards as a "wimp."

Chris is a vegetarian, but eats eggs and dairy, for which he feels very guilty, even though he spends extra money and buys cage-free eggs. Although he feels compassion for animals, he never pressures anyone else on the subject and doesn't join an animal rights group. Every Thanksgiving there is tension at Chris's parents' house because she won't eat turkey. She claims to dread the holiday but secretly enjoys the attention. Her parents have never understood her, and this is her unconscious way of getting back at them.

Chris loves science fiction and fantasy like *Doctor Who, Firefly*, and *Buffy, the Vampire Slayer*. She has a small tattoo of a *Star Trek* insignia on the inside of her ankle, but is otherwise ink-free. Science fiction gives her hope and fires her imagination. She has little use for serious drama or literature, except maybe for the Brontës. Despite her occasional forays into tempestuous romance stories, however, Chris's idea of love is cuddling and going to the latest Hobbit movie together.

Chris has little serious ambition in life. He wants an interesting job in a friendly organization where somebody else does the planning and takes the risks. He may start the occasional side-project but never finishes it. Chris is a Pretender and wants to be entertained by life, not in a cheap way, but in the sense of exploring "neat" things. He might want to have kids someday, but is not yet ready to give up being a child himself.

Chris is a little hard to peg politically. One Chris might be pushed by her adolescent resentment of authority in the direction of libertarianism, and if so, she enjoys making snarky remarks about the inefficiency of the post office. However, a different Chris might be pushed by his ingenuous good will toward liberalism and its ideal of society as a nurturing family, an ideal that he will happily force down everyone else's throats, since he cannot see how any decent human being could disagree with his values. The bridge between these conflicting ideologies is their agnosticism, their pro-science attitude and their rejection of what they regard as convention in favor of ideas and sentiments they consider obvious enough for a child to see.

Despite the occasional snarkiness, Chris is the soul of decency, doesn't consciously play games, doesn't have a cruel bone in her body and is full of wonder, albeit of an immature kind. Her first "instinct" is always to play nice with everyone else in the sandbox. But Chris can't understand why other people are not like her. She pigeonholes people who don't share her "niceness" as "Blue Meanies" or as unfeeling. She doesn't "get" people who don't want to hug grown-up children, who don't think of *The Lord of the Rings* as deep, and who take ideas, art and life seriously. If you're not cute and quirky, then to Chris you're boring or stunted. In short, child primalists have no concept of an adult, except for the half-dead grown-ups you see shambling around shopping malls like zombies. And without the concept of an adult, Chris can't grow up to be one.

The latest manifestation of child primalism is the cultural trend known as "Twee," which reporter Marc Spitz defines as (among other things) having a "healthy suspicion of adulthood" and an antipathy toward coolness in favor of a rehabilitated version of geekiness or nerdiness. A great example would be how wide-eyed actress/singer Zooey Deschanel is commonly referred to as "adorkable."

In my opinion, Twee, despite its freshness, is in many ways a disaster, a manifesto for never growing up, a celebration of youthful confusion whose only answer to life's problems is vulnerability and kindness. Now, vulnerability and kindness are good things and we could all use more of them, but they are not fundamental solutions to our problems. To imply that they are is to devalue serious thinking. Twee and primalism generally are, as strange as it may sound, forms of pragmatism—they are opposed to fundamental answers in favor of piecemeal, oblique, feel-your-way-through-things pseudo solutions to life's problems. This approach can sometimes make for good storytelling, but it almost always makes for rotten philosophy.

Just as animal primalism blocks cultural progress, so does child primalism, although in a different way. Chris has enthusiasms but not fire, nor vision, nor ambition. Although people like Chris are usually productively employed, essentially they are consumers, not makers, of values. Americans, influenced by child primalism, have become more like, well, children, instead of builders, lovers, men and women. Child primalists are Pretenders, who base their fantasy of innocence and wonder on an image of *Homo sapiens* the Explorer, but the reality is usually Chris the Tourist, a person of surprisingly narrow tastes who likes collecting neat things but is not very critical about them and whose idea of creativity is making a steampunk costume. As sweet a person as Chris is, he still represents the debasement of intelligence. Further, by infantilizing them, Chris gives love, kindness and wonder bad names—he makes them seem juvenile, quirky, geeky.

Child primalists are not as immediately disturbing as the brutish animal primalists of course, but in the long run they may be just as dangerous. Where animal primalism threatens us with violence and sexual exploitation, child primalism threatens us with *Brave New World*, a place where everybody hugs everybody, where "concern" and "caring" are imposed on everyone by ever-more intrusive legislation, where everything is made "safe," and where people celebrate their sense of life with Disney, even as adults. Cubicle by day, Deschanel by night. The thought that all those men and women toiled and died in the Revolution, the Civil War and WWII just to bring us to today's America is almost too much to bear.

I was a bit of a child primalist when I was younger, so I know it is possible to grow out of it, but you have to challenge yourself, you have to constantly look for better things that will broaden your horizons—and you have to be sensitive to the cheesiness of some of things you currently love, so that you can leave them behind or at least "bracket" your affection for them with the irony of nostalgia. It's not enough to go from "neat" thing to "neat" thing, like walking on stepping-stones across a lazy river. Sometimes you need to brave the torrent.

The reader may wonder why I'm being so hard on the primalists. I take no delight in being so. Although many animal primalists have distressing attitudes toward sex and power, many others are charming in a roguish sort of way. And child primalists are generally harmless and cute, despite their tendency to gang up on people politically. But these characteristics are not sufficient for adult human beings and someone needs to say so. People today are so afraid of "judging," that they don't want to criticize others, even when those others are hurting themselves and society.

And primalists are hurting themselves and society. They are substituting seriously impoverished fantasies for reality, with all the disastrous consequences that entails. Many of them think life is about satisfying something needy inside themselves instead of getting something magnificent done outside themselves. It's better to build a house, write a play or plant a garden than to wallow in immature feelings. This neediness becomes almost solipsistic as they try to appease their horniness and power-lust, or their need for warm fuzzies and gee-whiz spectacle. Furthermore, primalists generally lack ambition when it comes to self-improvement, because they believe their values cannot grow. They seek out art that is beneath them. They often do not have healthy adult romantic relationships. The animal primalists are too aggressive and the child primalists are too "nice." This is just not how human beings are meant to be.

Perhaps I should go a little easier on primalists, because our culture provides so little in the way of rational heroes to look up to that primalism may seem to be the only game in town. But even with this mitigating factor primalists have a serious offense on their heads: They have bought into a way of being based on half-digested snatches of science and philosophy, media role models and immature values. People can do better if they drop the ego satisfactions, get centered and stop Pretending.

People have created such fantasy complexes as primalism throughout the ages. For example, a Medieval boy might cobble together ideas from the Bible and troubadours, plus his own fantasies of gallantry and derring-do and dream of being a knight. Today it would be a Jedi knight or an alpha male. But with today's level of schooling and sophistication, the intelligent and/or educated primalists ought to know better than to buy into the theories behind the fantasies. It isn't that hard to say "I don't know," or "What else is there?" or "Does that always apply?" One doesn't have to be a philosopher to avoid egregiously bad ideas.

Primalism is a tragedy at the level of the individual

and a potential calamity at the level of society, where primalist fantasies contaminate policy decisions that ought to be made purely according to reason. The Iraq War was largely a result of animal primalism (Think of George W. Bush's macho war cry: "Bring it on!") and Obamacare was largely the result of child primalism (Think of the Democrats passing a bill they hadn't read—a colossal act of wishful thinking in the name of "sharing."). America is nearly bankrupt: We cannot afford mistakes of this magnitude anymore.

I don't want to overstate the culpability of the primalists. Individual primalists are not to blame for the state of the culture, of course, but I would hold them accountable for not using their imaginations and considering alternatives to their pet lifestyles. We can do better, both individually and as a society.

The Person of Principle

Fortunately, many, probably most, Americans are not primalists. They believe in principles rather than hungers as the justification of action, even if they don't understand those principles in a very sophisticated way. Let's look at an example of such a person, keeping in mind the wide variation possible within the type. The truly rational person—let's call her Susan—has a life plan, but it is based on secular reality. Susan has just left college. She had a good time in school. She studied graphic design, learning to create images that communicated a message, that were fun and that at their best, were original and beautiful. When she wasn't studying, she stretched, trying new music, dancing, and exploring the woods in the hills above the university, drawing pictures of the rock formations she found there. There was some pressure from her peers to drink or use drugs, but she was never tempted. She could tell at a glance that she was having a better time than they were.

Susan's basic policy, which has shaped everything about her, is that you can't just let things happen to you. She has seen her father, who is an animal primalist, destroy his life pursuing his pleasures, and her older sister, who seems to be a child primalist, is in the process of piddling her life away, barely scraping through college, desultorily going through the motions of applying to grad school because she doesn't know what to do with herself, while her pot-smoking boyfriend sponges off of her.

This is not for Susan. Susan knows what she wants: she wants to be creative in her field and to have a passionate marriage that includes children. She looks upon these things as part of the Good Life, a concept she learned in a philosophy class, where the professor used the Socratic method and taught her critical thinking. She knows that she has to be a certain kind of person to get these things: she has to plan and think outside the box, to see things through, to never settle for less while being realistic about what is possible. She knows she has to be honest and keep her promises, but that she should not let others take advantage of her. She has been cultivating these qualities since she was a little girl and is fairly self-conscious about them. Even though she's only 23 and is not fully formed, she has character.

To achieve her ends, she has channeled her artistic

talents into a field in which she could work at home, so she could run her own business while raising kids. She is engaged to Ben, a man she met in a class senior year. She finds Ben very attractive, but perhaps just as important, she respects him. He is reasonable and never plays games. Whenever they have a conflict, which isn't often, he patiently works with her and takes it apart so that they can both see their options. And he has a wonderful sense of humor, wry and dry. He reflects what Susan wants in life and she knows he would be a wonderful father. When they are alone and look at each other, they feel a desire mixed with wonder, because each sees a person who is focused, who is whole and who sparkles. Their friends are in awe of them and are inspired to try for what they have.

If there were more Susans and Bens in America today, we would be a lot better off. Neither of them is a Pretender or a primalist. Neither of them would have jumped on the bandwagons of the Iraq War or Obamacare. They would have demanded more thought on each subject and would not have allowed themselves to be bullied into supporting such measures. Nor does either of them like the general snarkiness and goriness of popular culture. Both recognize the virtue of cultivating one's ideas and sensibilities throughout life. Susan is doing some work with digital art on the side and she has already left the Dungeons and Dragons aesthetic typical of that medium far behind.

Susan is not a philosopher, of course. Her principles are not perfectly explicit, and she has not traced them down to their philosophical roots. This is a vulnerability in today's tumultuous culture. But she does live a life of reason, even if she does not put an "I ♥ Reason" bumper sticker on her car.

Thinking about Values

People do have hungers and felt needs—the primalists are right about this. Hungers are what small children base their actions on and felt needs tell us to some extent what is good for us as adults. For example, you know you need companionship because you feel lonely. Our inborn hungers are the starting point of value formation, and they no doubt color and constrain our adult values. But the primalists overlook four things about how hungers and values work that undermine their worldview.

First, as people leave infancy behind they begin to act on reasons, not hungers per se. Furthermore, as we grow up and our ability to see abstractions and the future grows, we develop a need to justify our actions—and these justifications have to be at least implicitly philosophical, because we cannot ignore the bigger picture we begin to see as we grow up. The philosophy involved can be quite implicit and simplistic, but it will still be a philosophy of sorts. The philosophic principle may be "because I feel like it," but that is still a reason. The person whose reason for acting is "because I feel like it" is at some level thinking "because feelings are what justify actions," and when others do not feel as he does, he very likely buys into some subjectivist theory like "That's true for you, but not for me." The variants of primalism are just such simplistic philosophies, supported by fantasies and cultural role models and dumbed down bad science and philosophy. But one could develop a good philosophy as well, based on common sense, discussions with friends and teachers, and things one has read.

The second thing about values and hungers that primalists overlook is that our hungers are not static. They become more sophisticated and find new objects as we age. A child's idea of sex is just rubbing herself, but that urge and that pleasure develop into a desire for contact with another human being whose vision of life complements her own, since this heightens and completes the pleasure. Freudians make the mistake of claiming that somewhere in the dark our desires persist in their infantile form. Not so. There is no substrate of "polymorphic perversity" underlying our adult values, if they are healthy. Our hungers develop along with our minds and bodies.

Some readers may think that I am proposing that reason "master" the emotions and "put them in their place." This is not the case. If we grow as we should, then the "natural" hungers and pleasures, in their developed forms, are incorporated into the reasons we base action on, providing needed energy and enthusiasm. When the transition to an adult mode of functioning is successful, the physical and psychological aspects of a value are combined with the cognitive and evaluative aspects so that there is no conflict, but rather a synergy. Reason tutors the hungers; the hungers impassion reason.

The third thing primalists overlook is that through reason a person becomes aware of values not directly comprehensible at a child or animal level, values such as long-term health, career, marriage and, indeed, life itself. For example, children are not aware at an early age of the issue of their own life and death. It is a conceptual discovery, and it gives rise to new, conceptual-level values and desires. And if anything helps a rational person integrate her values into a consistent, achievable vision, it is holding her own life as her highest value. Life as a rational being forms a standard by which our basic hungers, which all aim at life in a preconceptual way but which can easily become misdirected and contradictory, can be helped to find their proper objects and be put in the proper hierarchy. Using our conceptual knowledge, we can create an integrated life of passion and purpose, demonstrating that we are meant for a joyful existence here on earth.

The final pertinent fact that primalists overlook is the role ideas play in value formation. Values just aren't a given: although developmentally based on our hungers, they take the form they do because of our beliefs—and those beliefs can be false as well as true. Beliefs can be illusions, like religion. They can be fantasies, like primalism. They can be neuroses, as an irrational upbringing can cause. One of the chief tasks of philosophy, and of its allied field of psychology, is to remove such impediments from our sight so that we can understand what is really good for us. Despite their serious failings, many Americans in the eighteenth and nineteenth centuries had a fairly firm grasp of the reasoned life, and of course many people hold a kind of common sense version of it today, but many, many people are touched by primalism and pragmatism in their various forms. This contamination—and that is not too strong a word for the influence of the likes of Freud—has led people to live out unwholesome fantasies of casual sex and power or adolescent rebelliousness and spurious solidarity and to miss out on the pleasures of a rational purpose and an adult sense of wonder.

In conclusion, people do not and should not stay children forever, and if we are animals, we are quintessentially rational animals. However much we owe to our animal or child past, we have become something else, something novel in the universe. I am not suggesting that we deny our hungers or needs. I am suggesting that we realize that our hungers and needs are part of a larger economy of the soul, one which is guided by reason, but which has room for a healthy and appropriate satisfaction of our desires as they mature in a rational, yet passionate, context. The life of a rational person is not that of a child or animal. It is the self-realization and self-perfection of a fully human, adult being.

Justin

This essay is the follow-up to "Sex and Power, Hugs and Wonder," and they should be read in order.

It would be nice if we could get a handle on the salient American personality of our time now, rather than in hindsight a generation from now. To this end, I offer a short short story about a 24-year-old boy, a story that I call "The Last Day in the Life of Justin LaDouce."

Justin rolled out of bed late on Friday morning, having slept through his phone alarm again. He had been up late the previous night playing World of Warcraft and was quite tired. When he checked the time on his phone (he owned neither a watch nor a clock), he realized he was late for a meeting at work. No time for cereal, so he chugged two cans of Red Bull for breakfast and headed out the door.

Justin was a marketing manager for a local pizzeria chain called Pepperoni Palace. "Marketing manager" meant that he was a junior salesman, who did little more that stuff menus into door jambs, but it let him pay his parents some token rent on the semi-finished basement room he occupied since his mom, having thought he was gone for good, turned his old bedroom into a sewing room. It wasn't much of a job, but at least he had a job, which was more than most of his college classmates could say.

Justin had a degree in English from a good school. His bachelor's paper was called, "The Heart is a Lonely Reactor: Iron Man, Metallo and the Seat of Emotions." He had received an A- for the paper and he could still remember his adviser's comment on his work, "A significant exploration of the tropes of American comics. Add some insight into manga and you will have the basis for a dissertation." Driving to work, Justin mused dreamily as he remembered these words, thinking about how he would someday be a star both in academia and on the comic book convention circuit—that is, if he ever got around to studying for the GRE. He snapped back to reality just in time to avoid swerving into oncoming traffic.

Justin got to work an hour late, only to find his things in a cardboard box on the floor next to the desk that he shared with the senior menu stuffer, who said to him without looking up, "Strike three, bitch. Be fleet on the street." Justin picked up his box, made sure that his Terminator bobble-head was intact and walked out. "I'm too good for this effing job anyway," he proclaimed to no one in particular.

While driving to Dunkin' Donuts to get a proper breakfast, Justin texted a girl he had been trying to hook up with: "Sum1 wants 2CU. Hwbt 2nIt?" Then he unzipped to snap a picture of the "sum1." The light wasn't very good, and he was having trouble with the angle. He heard a very loud horn and looked up. The semi was the last thing he saw.

This is a caricature, of course, but millions of Americans do have something of Justin in them: too hooked into electronic devices, oblivious to reality, narcissistic, infantile, into symbolic aggression, inappropriately sexualized, dangerously in love with selfies. Although the cluster of characteristics as a whole is most common among people in their teens and twenties, I've seen some of these traits in people in their forties, fifties and even sixties. What is going on with the Justins of this world? Can we understand them enough to help save them from themselves?

The twenty-first century Justin is the son of twentieth-century animal and child primalists. They are a single lineage, although the species has evolved to fit in its modern high-tech environment. You can see both of the major variants of primalism in Justin's features. The symbolic aggressiveness of video games and the crude sexuality of sexting comes from the animal variant. The flightiness of his irresponsibility and the desire for attention of his selfies comes more from the child variant. The narcissism could come from either. However, as I said in the previous essay, these variants are not carved in stone. They are more like clouds that drift together or apart at different times and in different people. My sense is that the animal and child forms of primalism tended to be more separate in the twentieth century and are somewhat more merged in the twenty-first, as the process of cultural trickle-down reaches its ultimate puddle.

It's easy to believe that the roots of the Justin phenomenon are only 10 or 20 years old, because the Worldwide Web, the smart phone and other media developments are only that old, but actually the changes we are seeing in the American personality, although brought to a new level by recent technologies and applications, started decades earlier. Writers from Marshall McLuhan to Nicolas Carr have told us, half in warning and half in celebration, that modern media are reshaping the mind. I think that they are telling us only part of the story. It's true that the media shape the way we think, but it is even more true that what we think shapes the media. And one of the major thoughts that has shaped modern media is primalism. Let us turn now to some examples of this shaping, so that we can better understand the unnatural habitat of Justin and those like him.

What's on TV?

The last twenty years have seen startling advances in media technology: faster computers, the Internet and the Worldwide Web, the iPod, the smart phone, the e-reader and tablet computers. Yet some of the biggest changes in the media have been in an old technology: television. There have been enormous changes in TV programming in the last generation or so, with the rise of serial drama, such as *The Wire,* reality TV, talent contests, therapy TV such as *Dr. Phil,* court TV and "true confessions TV" such as *Jerry Springer.* Some of these genres have been around for a while, but have become much more commonplace and well-produced.

Television has reached new highs and new lows simultaneously.

"Reality" TV is probably the biggest new thing. These shows purport to capture "ordinary" people in spontaneous situations. Some are complete put-ons, such as *Duck Dynasty,* which involves scripts and costumes, while others portray people being somewhat like themselves and improvising part of the material. For example, many reality TV shows work by throwing strangers together, either into a lifeboat situation, such as *Survivor,* or into a mock circle of friends, such as *The Jersey Shore.* Then we watch them go at it. But is there any reality to reality TV? Even to the extent they are improvising rather than working off of scripts, the contestants or stars or whatever they are, are performing, trying to get attention and to manufacture drama. They are strategizing and putting on tactical displays of loyalty, temporary affection, backstabbing and the like. It's a queasy mixture of game-playing, acting and simulated sincerity, all of which require a primalist proxy self, usually of the animal variety. The overall tone is voyeuristic and gossipy, with all the stagey emotions of soap opera and the machinations of junior Machiavellis.

These shows would never have caught on if viewers weren't interested in seeing proxy selves on display, and viewers probably wouldn't have been interested in seeing that if they didn't believe in attention-seeking, acting out their emotions and melodrama as a way of life for themselves. As a friend of mine observed, a lot of young people today live their lives as if they were on reality TV, meaning that they *perform* their lives like soap opera, having seen "real" people do the same on television.

Reality TV did not create the desire for primal values such as attention and manipulation—in fact, the reverse is more nearly true. But watching reality TV gives young people like Justin a template for how to act out their lives. People get their strategies for living from *somewhere.* The term "television programming" has always had a double meaning.

Reality TV is a fairly easy target. A more difficult and disturbing phenomenon is the "therapy show," such as *Dr. Phil.* I think Philip McGraw means well, but by letting his guests put their troubles on display he is encouraging them to degrade themselves in the manner of child primalists. On one show a couple talked about how the wife had miscarried and how they lost a later child due to a childhood disease and how all this drove them apart. Can you imagine sharing your private agony with an audience composed of gooey "concerned" people, vultures, voyeurs and folks who just want to be entertained? I don't see how someone could do this without holding a fantasy in which one is a sensitive person surrounded by supportive, sympathetic people. This kind of misplaced openness and trust is characteristic of the child primalist, who tends to see life as a big group hug. Furthermore, like a lot of self-help, therapy TV pushes one to perform one's problems, dumb oneself down, go out of center and treat one's inner workings in the third person. ("Oh gosh! I'm stuck at the second stage of grief! Let's ask Dr. Phil what to do!")

TV and the Internet have also made celebrity gossip more widely available than they were in the old days of just *People* and *The National Enquirer.* You can't go to Yahoo's homepage without having it heaped upon you.

Celebrity gossip reduces its objects to little more than animals—who's cheating on whom? how does she look in a bikini? who was in a catfight on the red carpet? You'll never see a gossip headline that says, "Jen brushes up her craft to play Lady Macbeth."   People who find this sort of nonsense edifying are obviously primalists themselves, at least vicariously.

Listening for the Echo

Social media such as Facebook, Instagram and Twitter, as well as some blogs, encourage primal values in people. While social media are not instruments for satisfying primal needs such as possessions or sex (well, not for most people), users do strive for primal goods such as "childlike" wonder (in the form of cat photos or weird science stories); attention and popularity; and a kind of sway over others in the form of "likes," friends, and followers. There's even a web-based tool for measuring your online influence, called Klout. What the social media share with reality TV, therapy shows and the like is that all tend to entail a need to advertise and display oneself using a proxy self and acted-out emotions. Of course, social media are not primal in the most brutish sense, because, on the surface at least. they are more about sharing than competing. You could say that social media are primalism with a smiley face.

There is often a dubious oratorical quality to Facebook, Twitter and blogs. One talks about personal things to everyone in general—or to no one in particular, which amounts to the same thing. But communications without personal contact, without intimacy, are performances—not just for the phantom audience on the other side of the screen, but for oneself. One sends forth a proxy self, not necessarily the most cynical kind intended to manipulate others—more of an avatar designed to represent oneself. The danger here is that one might *become* one's avatar. The proxy self that one puts up on social media is often expansive, entertaining, ironic—a "look at me," theatrical self, hyped and participating in a social milieu that is profoundly unnatural. If I have a conversation in person or on the phone with someone, I generally have that person's complete and undivided attention, but on social media I am competing for many little fragments of attention. It's more like hanging out with a group of teenagers, whose attention one can only grab by saying wild things and making funny noises. That most people do not see this situation as problematic is due at least in part to the giddiness of technological triumphalism: We are drunk on the latest device, app or site, and we mostly don't think much about how, or even whether, we should integrate it into our lives.

One's circle of "friends," sometimes numbering in the thousands, can form a group mind that one might take part in. This seems to be especially true in large groups with a lot of connectivity, where you get rapid-fire banter, riffing, linking and sharing of photos. The giddiness of the group mind is especially manifest when people carry out some misdeed and then put it on the Web—for example, 300 teenagers trashing former NFL player Brian Holloway's mansion, and then posting pictures of themselves doing so on Twitter. People publicizing their hijinks in the social media and then getting caught by their employer or the law is so common an occurrence as to constitute a running joke. I suppose we could just chalk it up to stupidity, to drunkenness or to not knowing how Twitter shares information, but I think the group mind is at work, too, first in the negative synergy of the misdeed ("Hey! Watch me dance on this table!") and then in the desire to "share" it and get their whole circle involved and excited, because, after all, nothing is fully real until you take a picture of it and send it to your friends.

I'm guessing that when these twittering little birds share their adventures, their social circle is for them the whole universe, the group mind in communion with itself, and they are not thinking about anyone else who might be listening in. All of this is only possible when values are looked upon in a primal way. People who derive their values from reason don't break into someone's house, get drunk, trash it, and then publicly post pictures of themselves doing so. That takes a special mindset.

I believe the authentic self can participate in Facebook with some work—but I don't see how one can possibly participate in Twitter or Instagram beyond a minimal bulletin-board level, because rational values cannot be fitted into 140 characters (including spaces). Blogs can go either way. The ethos of many blogs is that one regards oneself as being somewhere between being an expert and being a prophet, but this expertise is based on one's personal cachet rather than on credentials. Everybody wants to be the first to identify the next new thing so that they can be the center of the universe for 15 minutes.

I'm not saying that these developments in the

"blogosphere" are entirely a bad thing, but one must concede that they are open to abuse. Some blogs seem like little more than attention-getting devices, even as others offer well-crafted essays or picture galleries or the like and do not involve projecting a proxy self into the group mind of the world. Good blogs are among the joys of modern life, because they circumvent the traditional media's ossified opinions. It all depends on the spirit in which the thing is done.

While we're on the subject of computer-based media, I ought to say a word about video games. Video games can be of several types, for example, explorations of an environment, scavenger hunts, shoot-outs or combinations thereof. Enormous care is taken to create the virtual worlds of the game, which are sometimes beautiful. Some people spend as much as four hours a day playing them.

The values of the violent games are primal on their face (survival, kill him before he kills you, macho competition, etc.). Most seem to have no real conceptual content beyond "good vs. evil" (and in some games it is actually "evil vs. evil"). The non-violent ones are less troubling, but they are still problematic, because they serve up canned wonder and invite one to see life too much as play. Obviously playing video games in moderation can be fun and fire the imagination. But I don't think it would be unreasonable to worry that extreme gaming contributes to being a primalist or a Fast-Time Pretender. (See the essay "As Free as a Finch" for more about the dangers of living in a world full of stories.)

Naked Youth

The integration of phones, cameras and comput-ers has facilitated the practice of sexting, which is the telephonic transmission of sexual photos or text. Sex-ting began as a practice among high school students; however, the percentage of teenagers who sext is very much in dispute, with estimates ranging from 1% to 50%, depending on the study. The photos can involve any state of dress, although the most notorious exam-ples feature nude or semi-nude subjects.

Sexting has caught on in the adult world, where some now seem to think it's a part of courtship (!), but the practice is obviously more of a concern when it involves minors. Sexts are usually shared privately to start with, but teens (usually boys) often end up circulating these photos (usually of girls) around their peer group, causing embarrassment to the girl whose nakedness is on display. The paradox is that sexting and the increase in oral sex in high schoolers both to some extent represent attempts to delay intercourse and avoid disease. Things are not as bacchanalian as they were in the 1960s and 1970s. Today's kids want it both ways: they want hot sex lives and they want to remain STD-free "virgins."

The typical girl who sexts is not (as far as my read-ing reveals) actually ready to have sex with the boys she sends pictures to. The girl is not even ready to pa-rade around half-naked in front of the boy in person. She is trying to create a sexy and fun proxy self to get attention and affection, while maintaining a safe dis-tance. It is part of a game. I suspect that at some level the boys and girls think of their bodies as something they own, as a kind of party-venue, rather than as an aspect of the person they are. This is third-person primalist thinking par excellence. An integrated view of the self, with rationally derived values, would not separate sexuality from love, self-respect and adoration.

Sexting seems to me to involve a kind of giddiness that is beyond mere Fast Time. Perhaps I should say more about giddiness, since I've referred to it several times in the book. Giddiness is a state of flighty excitement that occurs when one allows oneself to be out of control because it seems like fun. Throwing your hands in the air on a roller coaster is a mild and harmless form of giddiness. Taking that one drink too many is a not-so-harmless form. Young men get giddy riffing on things in their cultural and social environment (Think of teenagers singing Queen's "Bohemian Rhapsody" together.) Giddiness is the trivialization of ecstasy, which is too serious a business for the primalist or Pretender to handle.

You do not have to be a Freudian to see how giddily erotic the use of a proxy self can be for some people. This is obvious in the case of sexting, but I think it can also be seen in other modern phenomena such as online user names. User names can create a sense of mystery. They allow one to say things one would never dare utter using one's true name, plus they help one to express one's pseudo sense of life by adopting an exotic *nom de net* such as Angel666. This can be as sexy as wearing a mask at Carnival, because assuming a pseudonym is one way of creating a persona, and personae are deeply erotic, because they control access to the self and the erotic is all about penetrating the many layers of the self.

While a little flirting and play-acting can add spice to life, sexting goes far beyond this, and the long-term psychological consequences of it cannot be good. It's too soon to say definitely what will happen to young sexters, but I would guess that they will relate to themselves as some variant of "party animals" and not as human beings with real depth and presence. No doubt romantic love will be difficult for them to achieve. Young women like this are all-too-common today: knowing, cynical, superficially self-satisfied subscribers to *Cosmo* (three articles per issue on how to sexually please a man). Ah, but the sexting girl will have *fun*—until some callow boy sends her pictures around to everyone at school and she gets slut-shamed, bullied or otherwise humiliated.

Life in America has become incredibly sexualized—not romanticized, not eroticized, but just plain sexualized, with hooking up and sexting, Miley Cyrus and twerking, yoga pants and thong bikinis. Many girls dress like prostitutes, and both men and women get tattoos and piercings like members of some barbarian sex cult. In his notorious hit song "Blurred Lines," Robin Thicke tries to seduce a girl away from her boyfriend by saying that the boyfriend tried to "domesticate" her when really she's an "animal" whose wild nature Thicke offers to "liberate." He also refers to the girl as a "bitch"—but in a complimentary way. The unexpurgated video shows vacuous models flouncing around topless, looking like perfect toys. The song and the video only received token outrage. The rap sensibility had already paved the way for it. America has been seduced by animal primalism and is lovin' it.

The Shifting Ground Beneath Our Feet

As I said earlier, the new media were created large-ly to cater to people who *already* believed in a certain worldview, and that worldview is primalism. This can be seen in several ways. We *already* believed life to be a darwinistic sport of treachery and misdirection; *Survivor* merely embodies that belief. We *already* believed that adult discourse is a drag—and behold, there's Twitter. We *already* believed sex to be a pastime that we can play at will, as long as we don't exchange bodily fluids, and sexting fits the bill. We were *already* narcissistic primalists and the phone camera and social media just make it possible to endlessly document ourselves. The media merely act to amplify and petrify what we already thought we wanted. The media sell things, as they have always sold things, by catering to our fantasies.

Modern media owe their implicit ideology to twentieth-century primalism. However, contemporary media do add two new elements to the mix: 1. They have sped things up, and 2. They have pushed things farther from reality than they already were.

That modern media have sped experience up is obvious. It can be seen in video games; in the fact that certain things you once would have had to read about (accounts of therapy, gossip columns), you can now see on TV or online; in the rapid-fire, short-burst conversation of Facebook, Twitter and texting; in blogs where one can publish one's thoughts without finding a publisher; and in the instant gratification of sending photos and sexts. Everybody's desk at work has a computer, and Wikipedia is our source for immediate knowledge. Life has become much faster; it is as if we all moved to New York City. There are obvious advantages to these changes, of course, but there are dangerous disadvantages, too.

The increased speed correlates with a greater removal from reality, both in that it encourages skimming and flitting attention, and in that the new and faster media are electronic, which makes them inherently more representational than older activities: Facebook and Twitter are but representations of real conversations, engineered to break exchanges into brief snippets and to provide canned emotions in the form of emoticons or text abbreviations (such as LOL). Dr. Phil's show is more of a representation than reading therapeutic vignettes is, simply because it is filmed before an audience, which makes the therapeutic encounter a performance. Video games are more of a representation than real games. We work in virtual offices. We're obsessed with photos. Reality TV is just plain unreal. Today's world is like one giant multiplex cinema, with a thousand screens of irreality.

The faster, punchier, more stylized world of the mediasphere sinks its electrodes directly into our brains, bypassing our normal mental processes, so that things in the media seem more genuine than slow, gray, real reality. The needs and ambitions of the primalist drive out those of the rational person, as bad money drives out good. Reinforced by the representational nature of modern life, primalism is part of a worldview that holds that people are solipsistic bundles of drives that cry in the night, begging to be fed, titillated and serviced. Primalists, because they are focused on internal needs instead of external goals, live inside their heads, where, without the fresh air of reality, unwholesome things grow. And on the pedestal of our age, from which Beethoven's idol of Joy has been ripped, there stands Kim Kardashian, famous for no good reason, "glamorous" with the aid of the knife, parading her dysfunctional family through the streets like some sort of beggars' circus.

The Uphill Battle

Human beings are the most wonderful things in the known universe. But we do have our problems. One of our eternal temptations is to take the path of least resistance. This might be humankind's greatest hazard, because our basic choice in life, the one that allows us to get anything done, is to focus our minds, to pay attention to the world and to be fully present in it. This choice requires a constant effort. It means following a path of greater resistance, on principle. Like choosing to stand up straight, it can become easier as it becomes habitual, but it never becomes effortless.

Holding primal values, especially as they are realized in modern media, paves the path of least resistance: It's just too easy to watch reality TV rather than look for serious drama or sophisticated satire. It's just too easy to surf the Web rather than read a book, take a walk or visit a friend. It's just too easy to play a video game rather than play Frisbee with your friends or your dog. It's much too easy to be Justin: shallow, narcissistic, sexualized without being passionate, unaware of his surroundings, irresponsible, giddy. A lot of people are tired and bored and jaded and give into the desire to be entertained and to get their strokes from text messages or "likes," because they think that's what life is all about. Primalism and the modern media form a compound—a drug that addicts the unwary and keeps them from developing their full humanity. Even many people who take the path of greater resistance when it comes to working hard for money or power are often still taking the path of least resistance in that they are avoiding the harder work of actually thinking about their lives.

I always like to conclude an essay by offering social solutions and home remedies for the problems I have described. But here the ultimate cure is more abstract. We need a philosophical theory that restores reason to its proper place in life. I discussed some of this in the previous essay, and I hope to make that the subject of another book. The core idea is that reason is not just a way of manipulating abstractions but a faculty that helps us develop our values. This view of reason would let us shed the unhealthy fantasies of Pretenderism, primalism and the other subjects of this book. More on this topic appears in the concluding essay.

If such a theory becomes widely accepted and enough people renounce primalism, then we will start to see some changes. I would expect people to be more present in their surroundings instead of living in the mediasphere. People might want to get out in nature more, rather than looking at "autumn porn" on Reddit. Folks might remember that real intimacy is a one-on-one, real-time proposition, not something that can be obtained "hanging out" on social media. And people might challenge themselves to find better, books, movies, TV and music. I don't think possible developments can be predicted in detail. I could make a billion dollars if I could anticipate how the media might adapt to a more reason-oriented populace. But the market does adapt to culture.

I understand that the possible future I am describing sounds utopian, that it may seem utterly implausible that something so abstract as a theory of values could cause the behemoth of social trends to swerve in its course. This impression is due to a failure to understand what caused those social trends in the first place. They are not the product of economic and technological forces as such—these forces are but the vehicles of the real causes, which are theories of philosophy and psychology, especially as they are transmitted by art. Convince enough of the right people of a better theory, and the behemoth will march in a better direction. If you don't believe this, think how different a place black people and women have in American society now from the one they occupied fifty or sixty years ago. This was achieved partly by legislation, but ultimately by moral persuasion. Primalism and our unhealthy connection to the media can be changed by persuasion as well.

But even before a better notion of reason in human life becomes widespread, I believe people can take measures against Justinism. The biggest one is to change one's habits of socializing. Spend more one-on-one time with friends and family, in person or on the phone. The phone tends to increase intimacy rather than decrease it, unlike most media, so it is an acceptable substitute for in-person contact. (Although I have my doubts about the possibility of achieving intimacy during a phone call made *in public*.) Try reaching out to people you only know online with a visit, a phone call or a Skype conversation. Also read books more and those blurb-y online articles with 250 words and ten pictures less. Set your standards higher, always push, always strive for something better, never settle for what you have—especially not for what you loved when you were a student. Get out of your own head and discover nature and history and using your body. There's a big beautiful world out there, and you're never going to see it if you keep staring at your iPad.

I'd like to end this discussion with a simile. The self is like a balloon. If you don't blow it up, it just lies there limp and uninteresting, shaped by random forces. But if you push your breath against its resistance, it grows, it takes on a definite shape, and it becomes fun to play with. Choosing reason's inspiration is like inflating that balloon: it takes work, but the rewards far exceed the effort.

The Vampire and the Last Man

To paraphrase Marx, there is a specter haunting the world, the specter of the vampire. The vampire is the anti-hero of our age, stalking today's culture in innumerable books, movies, TV shows and video games. What is it that people long for when they escape into these tales of the undead? To find out we have to examine not only the seductive qualities of these stories but also what they are an escape from.

As of the time of this writing, there are 1,814 movies, TV episodes and videogames on the Internet Movie Database with the keyword "vampire." The bulk of these followed the publication of Anne Rice's bestselling novel *Interview with the Vampire* in 1976. Only 52 of the IMDb hits are from all the decades before 1960, but in the 1990s there were 264, almost twice as many as in any previous decade. In the 2000s there were an astounding 698 movies, TV shows and video games about vampires. The year 2012 saw 64 such releases, and more are in the pipeline. (These numbers are somewhat inflated by individual episodes of a TV series sometimes being counted separately.)

Amazon's search engine revealed that there are 15,429 paperback books with the keyword "vampire." (I didn't count hardcover or Kindle, because I was trying to avoid overlaps.) Of these, a whopping 284 were released in December 2012 alone. Although quite a few of these were re-releases, that's almost ten per day, more than even the most devoted fan could keep up with. Apparently the presses now run red instead of black.

Unnatural History

The vampire archetype has evolved considerably over the centuries. Many of the vampires of folklore were mere revenants, more like the modern idea of zombies. They didn't have a lot of personality. The vampire-as-character was created in 1816 by Dr. John Polidori, who based him on his patient, Lord Byron. Needless to say, the noble vampire reached his apogee in 1897 with Bram Stoker's *Dracula*. Count Dracula became the standard of the Aristocratic Vampire type.

The paradigm shifted again in 1967 with Barnabas Collins, the protagonist of the gothic soap opera, *Dark Shadows*. Even before Louis, the mopey narrator of *Interview*, Barnabas was a reluctant vampire, with one foot in his coffin and the other still in the human world of love and family. The Brooding Vampire, embodied by Barnabas and Louis and currently by Edward in *Twilight* and Bill in *True Blood*, has made it possible for the audience to sympathize with the vampire, rather than simply wanting to see him exterminated. Where Dracula is basically a well-dressed predator, the Brooding Vampire retains his humanity.

As if sensing that the vampire-type had become too approachable, moviemakers created a fourth species of vampire, the Bad Boy. The Bad Boy type is usually a low-class sort of person seething with resentment and enjoying his power and cruelty. He lacks the Brooding Vampire's human heart, and he lacks the Aristocratic Vampire's veneer of sophistication. Although I am no doubt overlooking some 1960s exploitation flick about vampire bikers, this type seems to have hit the mainstream with the 1987 comedy-horror film *The Lost Boys*. There are of course other vampire types, for example, the Seductress Vampire and the Child Vampire, but the main kinds in modern stories have been Aristocrat, Brooder and Bad Boy, with the original revenant variety mutating into the zombie archetype, the transition being found in Richard Matheson's vampire novel *I am Legend*, which spawned George Romero's zombie film *Night of the Living Dead*.

Other, non-vampire characters regularly star in the vampire drama as well. There is the Unwilling Victim, generally an innocent female who suffers the draining unto death. This character-type now plays a somewhat smaller role than it did in Stoker's day, since a Brooder will lose sympathy if he stalks and kills an innocent. The Unwilling Victim has been to some extent replaced by the vampire's Lady Love. Sometimes the Lady Love is regarded as a reincarnation of a beloved from the vampire's mortal life. Sometimes she is the rather unusual girl next door, such as Sookie in *True Blood* or Bella in The *Twilight* Series.

The last of the major characters is the vampire hunter. This type was first realized in Abraham van

Helsing in Abraham Stoker's *Dracula* and has more recently shown up in *Abraham Lincoln, Vampire Hunter.*
(And the Biblical Abraham almost cut his son's throat.
Hmmm.) The most famous modern hunter has to be
Buffy, the Vampire Slayer. Hunters are not as common as they once were—*Interview* does not have one
and neither does *Twilight* (at least not the first movie, which is as far as I could stand to go). If you make
vampires powerful enough, it becomes implausible
that mere humans could take them on, which is perhaps why so many stories today involve vampire vs.
vampire or vampire vs. werewolf conflicts. Perhaps to
counter this trend, hunters such as Buffy and Blade
are endowed with superhuman powers.

The Allure of the Undead

Fans by and large seem to identify with one or more
of the five main vampire-story archetypes: Aristocrat,
Brooder, Bad Boy, Lady Love or Hunter. These types
are embedded in a constellation of appealing qualities. The main ones that they possess are Atmosphere,
Superiority, Coolness and Passion.   Perhaps   we
can understand the popularity of the vampire story by
examining these attributes and what they represent
an escape from.

The vampire world is nothing if not Atmospheric.
Fangs and red eyes and dramatic swoops fire the imagination. Although vampire stories are generally frightening and bloody, they rely on mood more than most
other horror subgenres do and are typically less gory
and disgusting than most monster movies. Think of

the bloodless killing scene in *Le Théâtre des Vampires* in the film version of *Interview*. The stylishness of the vampire tale at times almost makes it transcend the horror genre.

Secondly, the physical Superiority of the vampire and, more recently, the hunter, is a big draw. Vampires have supernatural powers, notably great speed and strength. They are afterimages of Superman, right down to the cape that some of them wear and the arbitrary weaknesses that some of them possess (sunlight, instead of being the source of their strength, is their kryptonite). Male fans wish they were so strong; female fans want to be seduced by someone so strong.

The vampire's physical superiority can be seen as a symbol for a kind of class superiority. Some vampires are literal aristocrats, like Dracula, or at least members of the gentry, like Louis and Barnabas. Buffy is part of a long lineage of slayers. Bad Boys are not noble, of course, but they make up for it with an arrogant attitude. (Bad Boys, who are common on *True Blood*, are the rockers of the supernatural realm, and to the extent fans identify with them, they gratify the fans' resentment of authority figures.) Fans seek a kind of majesty through Aristocratic and Brooding Vampires, their Lady Loves and Hunters, majesty based on power or derring-do, but notably *not* based on achievement, except perhaps in the case of the Hunters.

The third appealing attribute of vampires and their entourage is Coolness. Most vampires are clearly cool, being mostly aloof and graceful—and they certainly defy convention. Hunters today are usually cool in a ninja sort of way, as in the case of Buffy and her gymnastic attacks and Blade and his amazing arsenal. (The traditional Hunter, such as Van Helsing, was not cool but was seriously square, a fact I will comment upon later.)

Like many cool people, the Aristocrats and some of the Brooders are clearly aesthetes of a sort. This makes sense because vampires do not work and usually have no family, and if you subtract work and family from life, most of what is left is the aesthetic element and/or romance. A lot of cool people wish they didn't have to work so they could spend more time cultivating their wardrobes. Well, vampires don't have to work, and their wardrobes are generally quite classy.

A fourth and final appeal of the undead and their traveling companions is Passion. Passion doesn't mean just sex (and many vampires don't have sex, anyway); it means any deeply felt emotion. Look at how vampires typically stalk their prey—with intensity and the utmost seriousness. Male sexuality is here often sublimated into a kind of predatory seductiveness: The vampire must ask permission to enter the house. He hypnotizes his intended with his eyes. He is strong; she is swooning. He wraps his cape around her and lays her down. Then the transaction is consummated. No doubt many women in real life wish their men would sublimate their sexuality a little more!

But passion in the vampire world goes beyond sexuality, sublimated or not. Vampire stories always involve urgent life-or-death conflicts, and these conflicts typically involve finding or saving someone you love. When in the case of some versions of Dracula, such as the ones starring Jack Palance and Gary Oldman, the count sees the character of Mina as a reincarnation of someone he loved when he was alive, we are contemplating a devotion that has lasted for centuries. The willingness of a vampire to risk his immortality for love signifies a passion beyond prudence. Here we see the Aristocrat taking on some of the characteristics of the Brooder.

An Unholy Sum

Why are the undead so popular at this moment? What makes so many turn to something so dark as vampires? Part of the answer is that for some, in the wake of the Holocaust, the epidemics of mass and serial murder, the alleged imminent extinction of humankind due to environmental degradation and all of the other horrors we daily dwell upon, God seems to have turned his back on us, and reason seems futile, merely a bad joke, a source of nuclear weapons and global warming. This world seems a storm-swept place "where ignorant armies clash by night." Vampires and their hunters help some people feel at home in that world, a world of Nazis and serial killers and pedophile priests that we rub each others' noses in every day. We teach children to make friends with murderers, through Count Chocula (a cereal killer) and the Count on Sesame Street. What's next—the Ted Bundy action figure? Murderers (including vampires) have gone from something too awful to discuss in polite company to being stock figures in our cultural world. Killing is fun! Watch *Dexter* if you don't believe me.

No doubt a number of fans of vampire books and movies are in it purely for the terror, the grotesquerie and the perverse sexuality, and some stories cater especially to those interests. But I think it would be safe to say that most fans are interested in the undead for more "human" reasons. It is a truism that science fiction, fantasy and horror are escapist genres, but what are the vampire lovers trying to escape from—and to? They're not trying to escape the storm-swept world because they are comfortable there. No, other factors are at work here.

At the risk of sounding Hegelian, I would ask the reader to consider the antitheses to the four points of attraction mentioned earlier. The opposites of Atmosphere, Superiority, Coolness and Passion are the Mundane, Vulnerability, Squareness and Prudence.

And what in today's world is Mundane, Vulnerable, Square and Prudent all at the same time? *The middle class lifestyle.* I would argue that the fan of vampire tales is trying to escape, in fantasy, the bourgeois way of life. Not just ordinary life or the mundane life, but specifically life under capitalism. The progression of vampire types reflects this attempt. Once upon a time we had the Aristocratic Dracula, who threatened the middle-class lives of Stoker's characters; now we have a James Dean-like Brooder like Edward who rescues Bella from middle-class boredom. This development perfectly sums up the evolution of the vampire tale. And Bad Boys are like Marlon Brando in *The Wild One*, subverting ordinary lives in their cocky, yet sexy, way.

The negative view of middle-class life has been popular in Western culture for more than a century, and not just among vampire lovers. I would suggest that the vampire fan is implicitly buying into the view of bourgeois existence originated by Friedrich Nietzsche (1844-1900), probably without having read him. For Nietzsche the middle-class person is heading toward an evolutionary dead end called the Last Man. The Last Man is a figure from Nietzsche's masterpiece *Thus Spoke Zarathustra*. He is the man who has no tension in his bow, no creative chaos in his soul. He cannot conceive of anything larger than his petty concerns. He avoids conflict so much that he never takes a stand on an important issue. Maybe he drinks a little to help him sleep, but not too much. He doesn't get too passionate about anything, because one must watch one's health. According to Nietzsche, all of bourgeois society is tending in this direction: a giant herd with no shepherd. Anybody who feels different will have himself committed. If you want a concretization of Nietzsche's view, Aldous Huxley created a futuristic world of Last Men in his dystopian novel *Brave New World:* banal, hedonistic, consumerist and free of conflict.

Many other critics have attacked the banality of the bourgeois, e.g. H.L. Mencken, Sinclair Lewis, C. Wright Mills, Christopher Lasch and, of course, sundry Marxists and feminists. People who have never heard of Nietzsche and the others can still tell you that middle class life is a "sell-out" that is shallow, cowardly and without passion.

Nietzsche talks a lot of master morality and slave morality and is sometimes taken as a champion of the master race, but that is not the case. He finds the type to be rapacious and shallow, although healthy in an animal sort of way. But he certainly does not care for the slave type, who believes in survival at any price. His hoped-for alternative to both master and slave is the overman (or superman, as the word used to be translated). The overman is the putative next stage in human development—not in physical evolution, but in cultural. The overman is a genius, an atheist, and a believer in mind-body integration. He doesn't let himself get swayed from his course by the claims of society or by pity. He is not a brute, but a creative child. Nietzsche thinks that we should all worship the overman and prepare a way for him.

The overman is a fantasy that serves Nietzsche as an alternative to the Last Man. The vampire-lover dreads the Last Man, but knows she does not have the kind of greatness Nietzsche envisioned for an overman. So she heads for lower ground: If she can't have the genius, she'll have the master. Most visions of greatness, including Nietzsche's, involve violence and domination. Napoleon is great. Alexander is great. Such things seem almost intrinsic to our notions of masculinity. And vampire lovers, male and female, want masculinity as opposed to the emasculation they see as part of bourgeois life.

The vampire aesthetic translates into master lifestyle most obviously in the elements of Cool and Passion. One of the defining characteristics of middle-class life is the concern with survival—the practical, as it's usually called. People tend to go along to get along and fit themselves into someone else's hierarchy. But the vampire and his retinue risk everything for Passion. One reason the Van Helsing type of Hunter has become obsolete is that he was a scholar, a middle-class man who restored bourgeois order and sanity to the world—and that is not what today's fans are after. The master type spits on mere prudence.

The Cool-loving vampire fan desperately wants to

say that there's more to life than middle-class appearances. One of the defining aspects of Cool, as Malcolm Gladwell has documented, is that it plays a little game of "I've got a secret and you can't guess it." Well, vampires certainly have a secret, and more importantly, the universe of the vampire story is portrayed as a covert underworld that the shopping-mall masses are blissfully unaware of until it reaches out and snatches one of them. The thought of this dark dimension to the world, known only by a few, makes the quotidian life bearable for the Cool person and allows him to look down on "normal people" as lacking his superior insight.

The vampire, in his Aristocratic or Brooding form, and the modern, super-human Hunter have a kind of majesty that promises greatness. Unfortunately, the vampire is the ultimate example of the false idea that what you are is more important than what you do—a kind of dark version of the Christian notion of salvation by faith and not good works. This kind of thinking leads to self-satisfaction because it does not require you to *do* anything. Such self-satisfaction translates to a love of luxury and hedonism. The vampire world consists of wenching, hunting, feasting and dressing up, just like the world of the old master race nobility. Imagine having hundreds of years of perfect health and not accomplishing anything! Most people who don't like middle-class existence haven't a clue as to what to replace it with except "sex, drugs and rock and roll." (Some of them do make art, but it is often pretty adolescent.)

It is probably not a coincidence that the popularity of the vampire story soared after the loosening of sexual morals in the sixties and seventies. Many people now believe that physical attraction alone is enough to justify sexual intimacy. (Oh, she has a nice neck!) By divorcing sex from love we have replaced courtship with a sub-rational, quasi-predatory sexual pursuit. This is why vampire sexuality fits so neatly into our world.

Not everyone can drink this potion straight, however. The seductive attack and the vampire's longing for his Lady Love allow some of us to bootleg an element of romance into the culture of sanguinary hooking-up. This move is contradictory, however, because the vampire is the epitome of promiscuity. Recent attempts to make him faithful are but the fantasies of teenage girls of all ages, who dream that their love is enough to capture a bad man's heart. And note that most of the popular vampire stories of today are female fantasies. *Buffy, Twilight* and *True Blood* have young women at their centers. *Interview* is almost entirely about men, but Anne Rice has said that she is in love with her creation Lestat, and I suspect she didn't want to share him with a female character.

All of this suggests that a large part of the dynamic of the vampire story is that many women are uncomfortable fitting themselves into capitalistic life and long for a return to a time when women were ladies, courted by knights. In the case of vampire lovers, these would be Dark Knights, the only kind permitted in our cynical age. Men on the other hand, get to identify with Bad Boys or ninja-like Hunters like Blade, which allows them to escape the bourgeois world, too.

If this hypothesis is correct, then two of the causes of vampire popularity are backlashes: first, against feminism, which strove mightily to kill chivalry, and second, against the integration of women into the workforce, which narrowed the difference between the sexes. These factors, along with the increased exposure to horrific things since the Holocaust, may well be a sufficient explanation of the torrent of red that threatens to flood the cultural countryside.

Putting a Stake Through Its Heart

Maybe nothing has to be done about the vampire story's growing popularity. Maybe we should regard vampire stories as just juvenile fantasies that will be outgrown in time. This may be true of the *Twilight* series, but too many adults love *Buffy* and *True Blood* to hope for that outcome, and other tales of the undead are clearly written for adults, such as *Anita Blake, Vampire Hunter* (which is erotica) and Anne Rice's *Vampire Chronicles*, some of which verge on literary fiction. We're not so easily going to escape from escapism.

Maybe instead we should just regard vampire stories as the new opiate of the masses, something to keep people who are never going to achieve greatness satisfied with their lot, something that functions like that beer and circuses known as professional sports. I can't accept such a cynical proposal, but I believe that the reader should ponder it for a few minutes and ask himself just why it would be wrong to keep people content and docile using fantasy stories.

Here's *my* answer: Vampire stories are patently unhealthy. They are about creatures that feel entitled to murder innocent people for dinner. The whole idea of drinking blood is disgusting. And the linkage of sexuality with predation is ominous, to say the least. People especially are surely taking the wrong messages about life and love from these tales. I would suggest that consuming vampire stories on a regular basis reduces empathy for others and that the idea of that what's important is what you are instead of what you do encourages one not to take responsibility for oneself, but just dream.

Yes, but couldn't you say that about all literature, film and TV stories to some extent? Aren't they all fantasy? Indeed they are. But vampire stories tend to compensate for frustration rather than illuminate life's problems. They do not connect with real life. This is not true of all fiction. If I watch *Mad Men*, for example, I am immersed in the fantasy of a world that no longer exists, but hat story sheds light on the present, sheds light on big questions about identity, men and women, and the function of advertising and commerce in American life. It puts me more into the real world, even though it is a fantasy.

Vampire stories, and genre fiction generally, don't connect me to the real world, but take me deeper into my own head, into the self-contained Bubble Universe of the Pretender. Over-indulging in this kind of fantasy is like conjuring ever more twisted masturbatory fantasies instead of seeking an intimate encounter with an actual person: Feeding feelings is given precedence over life in the real world.

To put the popularity of the vampire tale in context, we need to recognize that the biggest problem for America in modern times, at least since turning the tide against racism, sexism and communism, is how to reconcile ourselves to capitalism and middle class life. Vampire idolatry just tries to dodge the problem, by letting the fan flee into a world where there is no ambition, no family, no mortgage, and no quest for self-improvement. But the realities of capitalism and bourgeois life must be faced. They are not going away. Capitalism is the only system that can support the population of this nation and this planet at an acceptable standard of living. Feasting on a fantasy of the master race lifestyle, at least as more than an occasional bonbon, makes it that much more difficult to face facts.

And these facts need not be unpleasant facts. The path that reconciliation with capitalism must take is more the subject for a book than a single essay, but two broad strokes can be indicated. The first is that we need to reduce the amount of horror in the American diet, especially children's diets. Capitalism depends on a belief in a sunlit world full of positive opportunities. Populating that world with monsters makes it harder for people to believe that there are always possibilities. I am not referring just to imaginary monsters such as vampires and zombies, but also to real ones such as Nazis, serial killers, pedophile priests and the like. Material on these subjects is too widespread, too easily accessible. Whereas true crime and horror used to be marginal categories in books, movies and TV, they now appear on par with other forms of genre fiction. And much of genre fiction—not just horror, but thrillers and mysteries—is too often unspeakably repellent in its depictions of graphic violence. In addition vampire stories out-wuther *Wuthering Heights* in their moody depictions of anguish. The danger if you romanticize suffering is not that people will give up, lie down and die, but that they will try to adapt by becoming Dreamy Pretenders or masochists or even, God forbid, sadists. Note that *Fifty Shades of Grey*, the runaway indie bestseller about a woman who falls in love with a man who has a torture chamber, started out as fan fiction based on *Twilight*. And who do you think reads that stuff? Women who want a man from the master race.

Secondly, if we want people to stop running away from bourgeois life, we need to help them find what is worthwhile about that life. One might say, paraphrasing Churchill, that middle-class life is the worst lifestyle possible, except for all the others. But are things really that bad? The vampire lover sees middle-class life through a distorting lens. It isn't really about selling out; it's about building as high as you are willing and able to. The real defining characteristic of bourgeois life isn't really passionless squareness, but freedom, the freedom to do what you want as long as you let others do the same—including the freedom to acquire property.

As a corollary to these characteristics we have seen the growth of large organizations, with great economies of scale, which many people join. You don't have to be a Marxist to believe that selling your labor to an organization whose goals you don't personally care about can be alienating. One traditional solution to this problem, at least in American life, is to recognize that if the company prospers, you prosper (and it behooves a company to make sure this is true)—and to take pride in a job well done. This work ethic has been eroded over the last few decades, but surely it can be restored.

For those who do not wish to salute the corporate flag, the traditional solution has always been to open one's own business. This has become more difficult over the last few decades. The main reason for this is that our over-regulated, over-taxed system of crony capitalism, which favors large businesses, makes it very difficult for small ones to flourish. No doubt in a freer society, many disaffected people would leave their cubicles behind, turn off the TV and start their own enterprises. The cure for the Last Man, who is the ultimate cube-dweller, is not a fantasy about the master race but a purer form of capitalism.

As a corollary to this we must also craft a new ideal of greatness. Nietzsche's dream of the overman is not going to do the trick, because that dream is just a fantasy, only open to geniuses, unattainable for everyone below the level of a Julius Caesar or a Goethe. I'm proposing an ideal of greatness for hard-working, sensible people, not just brilliant people. And I'm not talking merely or even primarily about opportunities in business, but in all kinds of creativity and self-development. To borrow a phrase from the Christian author Rick Warren, we could call it a Purpose-Driven Life, but I mean Purpose in the secular sense of having a mission for organizing one's life, i.e. building something, whether it is a skyscraper, a restaurant, a garden, a body of writing or a family. (More about greatness in our concluding essay.)

When the vampire lover retreats into her fantasy world of masters and beloveds, she becomes passive. What she needs is to become active, i.e. Purpose-Driven. This is a difficult problem for many female fans especially, who feel torn between career on the one hand and romance and/or family on the other. I don't pretend to know the solution to this problem, but I can tell you than fantasizing about being seduced by a murderer isn't a part of it. Engaging the world and realizing one's potential in whatever sphere one chooses is a needed antithesis to reveries about Transylvania.

Purpose in this sense means developing yourself, even in what you do for fun. Much more could be said on this subject, but it is clear that this quest would include reading and viewing really good art—abandoning the vampires to their musty coffins and demanding something better, something living. To sum it up a little formulaically, the antidote to fantasizing about killers is to get off the couch and start building a dream. And if you want more eroticism in your life, take tango lessons. What we need is a new cultural sunrise that will start to cleanse the land of the undead parasites that have swarmed over it. If we can reduce the perception of darkness in the world and learn to see the opportunities in free, middle-class society, then perhaps the vampire will once again become the curiosity he used to be and cease to be a metaphor for our conflicted age.

Killing Cool

Like most of the classrooms where I went to middle school, my eighth-grade French classroom had a blackboard on both the front and the back walls. The desks were arranged in two banks that faced each other across a central aisle, in a style reminiscent of the House of Commons.

Some of the other boys in the class always tried to use the back blackboard, and I noticed one of them had written in small letters in the lower right corner

KGB

That was cryptic. I wondered what the infamous Soviet security agency had to do with irregular verbs. Eventually, I asked one of the backboard boys about it, and he informed me that KGB stood for Kool Guys Board and that only Kool Guys were allowed to write on that board. This did not impress me. I quickly dismissed the Kool Guys' attempts at self-aggrandizement as immature, although I was intensely jealous of their ringleader's impression of Boris Karloff.

This episode was my introduction to an important aspect of the phenomenon of Cool: the attempt to create superiority *ex nihilo*, i.e. out of nothing, as God supposedly created the universe.

It is easy to dismiss Coolness as merely juvenile. We might say to ourselves: "Who cares what shoes kids wear? Who cares which celebrity is in or out this week? Such things are mere chewing gum for unoccupied minds. When young people grow up, they'll move on to more serious things." Unfortunately, this is often not true. A lot of people don't grow out of thinking in terms of Cool. Furthermore, there are many other behaviors that are part of the various Cool lifestyles besides choosing footwear. And some of these behaviors can leave a life in ruins.

One such behavior is smoking. Smokers usually begin smoking when they are teenagers, and their decision to begin is typically influenced by the desire to look Cool. Given that tobacco is as addictive as heroin and that one in six smokers gets lung cancer (the same odds as in one round of Russian roulette), it would behoove us to take the cause of smoking seriously. And smoking is not the only serious consequence of trying to be Cool. The desire to be cool also plays a large role in drug and alcohol use, casual sex and an aversion to learning (as in "too cool for school"). In addition, it factors into questionable art movements such as modernism and post-modernism, and spawns a general shallowness. Given the wide collection of dire things that stem, at least partly, from the same cause, it makes sense to attack the root: *to kill Cool.*

Of course, this has been tried before. Ministers denounced Elvis. Public service ads entreated, "Just say no." Athletes have told young people to get an education. Maybe some of these tactics have worked to some extent—it's hard to measure results. (Elvis, fortunately, survived the castigation.) But the problem is that none of them got to the heart of the phenomenon, and all of them were so conspicuously *un*cool as to provoke giggling. If we want to change Cool-based behaviors, we must discover what Cool really is, why it exists, what partially good goal it is trying to accomplish, and what we can do to change the game.

Some readers may be taken aback to my hostility to Cool, which many people associate with fun, not destruction. If you are such a reader, I respectfully ask you to keep reading and be ready to challenge your assumptions, for it is the way we think that causes our problems.

A Pocketful of Cool

If you want to fight an idea, you must define it. People greatly underestimate the value of formal definitions and allow themselves to be hazy and impressionistic about the things that concern them. Pinning down Cool is notoriously difficult. Malcolm Gladwell spent an entire essay, "The Coolhunt," telling us that Cool is something that eludes your grasp every time you think you have it. If by that he means that we can't predict tomorrow's fashions, I agree, but if he means that we can't say what Coolness in the abstract is, then I don't. . But defining Cool won't be easy, because Cool isn't a superficial concept, despite its frequent obsession with superficial things.

To begin with, Cool isn't just one thing. Nietzsche said that a word is like a pocket: first you put one thing in it, then another, then many things at once. Speaking just of the meanings that have to do with style, the Cool "pocket" currently contains three big things. I call them Casual Cool, Vanguard Cool and Outsider Cool. To introduce the meanings briefly, Casual Cool consists of things you think are amazing; Vanguard Cool consists of trendsetting stuff and people; and Outsider Cool consists of stylish alienation.

First we need to dispense with Causal Cool, which is the kind of Cool that people perceive as innocent and fun. Casual Cool doesn't have much to do with the attempt to create superiority, which I am claiming is the heart of Cool. A good example of Casual Cool would be astronomer Carl Sagan. I've even heard Mister Rogers described as Cool in this way. Another example would be a website I found called "10 Cool Things You Can do with a USB Port." Hmmm. Back in the '70s we used to a have a word for things that impress us with their sunshiny ingenuity, and it wasn't "Cool." It was "neat." Really intense people used to say "nifty." Today people often say "Cool" when it would be more appropriate to say "neat. " For example, I might describe the latest innovation from Apple as "Cool," but what I really mean is "neat" (well, "nifty," actually). Calling something that you like in this manner Cool is usually just a way of borrowing the luster of the two hardcore meanings of Cool. Casual Cool doesn't have much impact on smoking and other dangerous activities and we will not consider it further.

The second item in the Cool pocket is Vanguard Cool, which is very popular today. Here a good classic instance might be Frank Sinatra or George Clooney or Miley Cyrus. Vanguard Cool is the Cool Malcolm Gladwell famously wrote about. It is the Cool of trendiness and fashion superiority and supporting chic political causes. The latest super-model is usually Cool in this sense, as are most designer shades. Baroque sneakers with Day-Glo colors are Vanguard Cool, but so are suits by P. Diddy or whatever we're calling him this week: Vanguard Cool is not just for kids.

The last and most interesting kind of Cool in our pocket is Outsider Cool. This is the gutbucket Cool embodied in James Dean and Kurt Cobain. Wearing black is Outsider Cool. Playing your trumpet with your back to the audience is Outsider Cool. Heroin is Outsider Cool. To the extent it concerns shoes at all, it's about wearing something that most people would think are unfashionable, like Doc Martens or Keds. Where Vanguard Cool tends to the ostentatious, Outsider Cool tends to the aloof and subversive, and each subspecies can be quite suspicious of the other.

But even though the two big kinds of Cool may have some conflicting attributes, they share a common core, which I've boiled down to four characteristics: 1. Stylism, 2. Competitiveness, 3. Esotericism, and 4. A fascination with popular culture.

1. Stylism means putting style above other values such as rationality, morality and benevolence. Both Vanguard and Outsider Cool people are obviously obsessed with style. Not just in things such as choice of clothes and music, but also in language and demeanor. As the late Navy SEAL sniper Chris Kyle stated, "Ninety percent of *being* cool is *looking* cool." Unlike many people traditionally concerned with aesthetics, Cool folk don't think that beauty is something they have to live up to. Rather, they regard the aesthetic dimension of life as something that exists to glorify them. This leads to—

2. Competitiveness. The point of hardcore Cool is to feel superior to other people. It's an ego satisfaction. Look at the sobriquets Cool people are sometimes given: Elvis was the King. Sinatra was the Chairman of the Board. Springsteen is the Boss. When something is very Cool, it "rules." Vanguard people compete to see who's trendier than everyone else. Outsiders try to prove that they're separate from and superior to society's standards.

Cool things are often "outrageous," such as hip-hoppers wearing their pants off their butts or Angelina Jolie's entire demeanor. The whole point of this outrageousness is to say, "Look at me. What I do subverts your norms, but I can get away with it, because I am Cool. You can't get away with it, because you're square, white, ordinary, scared, a geek, etc." But superiority has to be based on some kind of attribute, even if it is one as empty as royal blood. It can't be asserted baldly, except by narcissists and psychopaths. This leads us to—

3. Esotericism, which is the idea that the enlightened can see the important things in life, while everyone else is shut out. Think of it as the doctrine of hidden wisdom. Cool people believe themselves to have special insight into the Zeitgeist, about which more later. Other people are blind to Cool or at best pathetically imitate it. As Malcolm Gladwell writes, only the Cool know Cool. Lastly, every sport requires a playing field, and that brings us to—

4. A fascination with popular culture as the content of Cool. Cool people generally take popular culture far more seriously than it deserves. Although some Cool sophisticates have been known to love Rimbaud, Van Gogh and art house movies, the general lot is more interested in Kanye West, Portishead or this week's Nikes. There are, I believe, two mutually reinforcing reasons for this: First, Cool is cynical and believes in "primal" values of the animal variety such as sex, status and easy ecstasy, which are the values of popular culture. Second, Cool people need an "establishment" to rebel against, and popular culture typically positions itself in contrast with higher culture. For almost 60 years, the Cool theme song has been "Roll Over, Beethoven."

In addition to meeting these four criteria, a Cool person must of course be able to pull off the pose; one can't be a mere wannabe. Not that wannabes are bad to have around, however: The failed Cool person is essential to the ecology of Cool, because the Cool need the uncool to be superior to, and it's easier to score off of people who are playing the same game one is.

The Ghost of our Age

I mentioned the Zeitgeist a moment ago. "Zeitgeist" is a German word that means "the spirit of the time." For example, when someone refers to the 18th century as The Age of Reason, they are referring to its Zeitgeist. You can use the concept of the Zeitgeist in either a secular way or a mystical way. In its secular sense it just refers to the ideas and fashions of an era, which tend to be somewhat coherent thematically due to related developments in philosophy, science, technology and art. We might experience these developments as a kind of "feel" or Gestalt, but that is just our unconscious integration of loosely related material.

The mystical sense of the Zeitgeist is an alleged spiritual force—not a person, as God is supposed to be, but still supernatural and having an objective existence. It's a disembodied feeling, almost a sense of inevitability that hovers in the air and settles over things and people. Imagine that the universe has a sense of life that evolves according to some sort of master narrative. On this view, for example, the 1950s in America was a time of conformity, with superficial innocence masking hidden repression, leading inexorably to the rebellions of the 1960s. Its sense of life can be represented with a montage of clips from *The Man in the Gray Flannel Suit* and "Leave It to Beaver" and songs by Elvis, with snippets of Beat poetry thrown in. To people who believe in it, the mystical Zeitgeist of an era is a nearly irresistible force. For better or worse, it is the idea whose time has come.

This belief is what you might call pop-Hegelianism. The philosopher G.W.F. Hegel (1770-1831) believed that the great man was the one who tapped into the spirit of his age and gave it voice. If you substitute "Cool person" for "great man," you can see how hardcore Cool people think of themselves. Of course, Hegel meant Julius Caesar and Napoleon, where followers of Cool mean Bob Dylan and Eldridge Cleaver, but it's the same dynamic.

Cool people validate themselves by their relationship to the mystical Zeitgeist. In extreme cases, Cool people believe that they create or at least anticipate the Zeitgeist. The Vanguard Cool swim with the current of the Zeitgeist, setting fashions as they go. Think of mini-skirts or big hair or ties and shirts of the same color, to cite styles from three different eras. As dated as these things now seem, they were once the fashion of the times and one would appear hip for wearing them.

The Outsider Cool mostly swim in the undercurrents of the Zeitgeist. The undercurrents consist of darker, wilder, subtler trends that run contrary to the culture's dominant ideas and that allegedly give it greater depth and vitality. In keeping with their subversive nature, they are usually ironic. The premier examples of Zeitgeist undercurrents in America are black musical movements such as jazz and rap, but white people come up with their own material, too, such as The Velvet Underground and various kinds of post-punk music. Music is *the* art form of both kinds of the Cool, because music can simulate the experience of the mystical Zeitgeist, namely, a feeling that is compelling, diffuse and all around us.

Notice that trends can start out as Outsider and end up in the Vanguard: marijuana and multiple piercings of the ear would be two examples, but heroin and piercings of the lip are and probably will remain pure Outsider Cool. The Vanguard likes to be a little daring (Think twerking.), but usually is interested in a "normal" life. Transgressiveness is for them only a condiment.

It may sound incredible that people who are mostly interested in fashion superiority actually believe in a transcendent power, but I ask you to consider the evidence. The idea of the mystical Zeitgeist is common among Cool people and in American culture generally. Examples include:

- Our fascination with decades, such as the 1950s, mentioned before, or the Me Decade, the Roaring Twenties, the Big Eighties, etc. Each decade is regarded as a discrete "Zeit" that has its own "Geist."

- An obsession with slang and fashion. This usually has to do with not wanting to fall out of touch with the times. The extreme here is that slang cheat-sheet known as *The Urban Dictionary*.

- The sense many people have that something is "right" for the present moment. Barack Obama's slogans of "Hope" and "Change" played into a feeling of contacting the Zeitgeist directly. And weren't those Warholesque posters with Obama's face Cool? (The closest Republican equivalent to this was Reagan's campaign slogan, "It's morning in America.")

- Phrases such as "cutting edge," "wave of the future" and "being ahead of the curve" suggest that the Zeitgeist is an objective power in the world that one keeps up with or falls behind.

The Zeitgeist isn't the only spiritual but non-personal concept that's floating around. Karma, a belief that the universe metes out some kind of justice on us all, is another example. Luck, the belief that the universe smiles on some and frowns on others, is yet another. People even project their pessimism onto reality, as in

Murphy's Law. We may not believe in ghosts anymore, but many of us do believe the world is haunted. Concepts such as these falsify reality and thus falsify the self. If you believe "I am an unlucky person" or "I am a Cool person," you are not letting yourself be who you are, i.e. a person with free will living in a world that has no intentions toward you one way or the other.

The mystical concept of the Zeitgeist represents a common psychological phenomenon wherein we project something mental, such as a pseudo sense of life, onto reality and then believe we found it there. People often impute imaginary forces with inevitability in order to create a powerful ally in their personal struggle, like a guardian angel standing by their side. When the concept of Cool arose in its present form among African-American men living under Jim Crow, it helped them in their fight for self-respect in the face of humiliating oppression. They needed a self-image of grace, independence and moral superiority to their oppressors just to flourish. Then, Cool had survival value. Now, Coolness is a form of Pretenderism, just a tool for ego satisfaction. Think of rap and hipsterism.

The ethical problem with Cool is that you can't position yourself as superior without positioning someone else as inferior. Cool is a spiritual hierarchy, ordered by degrees of "enlightenment," with the hip on top and the geeks on the bottom. Despite its contributions to music and design, the Cool worldview is not only false but also hurtful. Fortunately, you can be passionate, creative, funny and self-confident all without being Cool, although Cool people don't want to admit this.

As I said before, in order to fight a phenomenon we need definitions, which we are now in a position to offer: "Coolness" is an attempt to achieve superiority in the realm of popular culture by means of alleged esoteric wisdom about style.

"Vanguard Cool" is Cool that is concerned with the leading edge of the mystical Zeitgeist and aims at being ahead of others in their pursuit of Cool. Outsider Cool is Cool that identifies with Zeitgeist undercurrents and takes a superior stance based on alienation from social and aesthetic norms. Now that we have definitions, we are ready to delve deeper into the effects of Cool and then to turn to causes and remedies.

How Cool Burns Us

It's easy to think that Cool is a phenomenon of superficial style mannerisms, just college kids listening to Death Cab for Cutie and getting funny haircuts, but this is not true. As I said earlier, Coolness has had far-reaching effects on the American soul, on adults as well as on youngsters.

First of all, there's substance abuse. I mentioned smoking and drug abuse before, but I didn't mention that approximately a quarter of a million Americans die every year from tobacco, alcohol and drug abuse and no doubt millions more have their lives reduced by heart and lung disease, alcoholism or addiction. How many people who will die or suffer in the next 20 years got hooked on tobacco or booze by the Joe Camel cigarette ads or the James Bond-style liquor ads of the 1990s, both of which embodied a kind of Cool? Young people do stupid things because they think such things make them Cool, and the market is shameless about exploiting that desire.

Second is TV. While what we are putting in our bodies is of vital importance, so is what we are putting in our souls. Many of the protagonists we watch on today's shows are not heroes or even interesting anti-heroes, but Cool misfits and monsters: vampires, serial killers, gangsters, outlaw bikers, middle-class folk become drug dealers/manufacturers, etc. Viewers don't take these characters as role models (I hope), but they do root for them, and the characters are glamorous in their savvy cynicism, their stylishness and their twisted superiority. (Think of Walter White in his Heisenberg persona in *Breaking Bad.*) Such morally compromised protagonists would have been almost unthinkable on TV even just 20 years ago, and one has to be deeply immersed in the culture of Cool not to see how problematic all of this is. It is a striking example of what Daniel Patrick Moynihan called "Defining Deviancy Down"—a recurring characteristic of Cool as it tries to stay on the cutting edge and maintain a high level of stimulation. These shows are the absinthe of our time, and it is impossible to believe that they are not having a harmful effect psychologically and spiritually.

Third would be tattoos, which have become quite common in the twenty-first century. I don't claim to understand the psychology of getting tattoos, but I do know a few things about them. First is that most of them look bad when they're new and all of them look bad when they're 20 years old. Second, the person getting inked clearly believes that butterflies, skulls, spider webs, flowers and other elements of comic book art are worthy to be immortalized on one's skin—that is to say, on one's soul. So we definitely see rampant stylism and fascination with popular culture. G o i n g out on a limb now, I would suggest that to put a picture or words on one's skin requires that one view one's body from a third-person perspective as an object one owns, rather than as the self that one is, and further-more, to get tattoos is to participate in some kind of tribalistic collective mind. If I am right about this, then getting a tattoo is not only an instance of Cool, but also an expression of primal values, with all the negative consequences thereof.

Fourth is the use of derogatory terms such as "geek" and "nerd." I don't mean just the way in which some jocks and frat boys use such language to humili-ate kids with glasses. I mean the way in which some intelligent people apply such terms *to themselves.* Some smart people use the terms mockingly or even proudly, as if humor will de-fang the language. In my opinion, this doesn't work; it just reinforces the un-derlying assumptions of the words, namely, that some people are right for the cosmos while others just limp their way through life looking ridiculous. It's just like rappers using the N-word: It buttresses the prejudice. What is called for is an overthrow of this pernicious social order. I wear glasses, am good at math and like *Star Trek*, and I would never let anyone characterize me as a nerd or a geek. I am too good for that, and so is everyone else.

Fifth is politics. Cool isn't just about shoes. At its most serious, Cool is also about knowing which cause is chic at a given moment. Needless to say, style is not a good criterion for choosing whom to support in the political sphere. Consider the case of conductor/composer Leonard Bernstein, looking very Cool in one of his signature black turtleneck shirts, helping to raise money for the Black Panthers in 1970. Beethoven sure rolled over that time! Many of today's left-wing causes, such as Greenpeace, also get a boost from being Cool. The right's idea of Cool is the Tea Party's "Don't Tread on Me" flags, which are too hokey to be really Cool. Conservatives are inherently anti-Zeitgeist, and so aren't very good at being Cool, although some of the conservative commentators try in their own awkward way. Needless to say, politics is far too important to be influenced by fashion.

Lastly, Coolness over the last few decades has been supplanting other categories of goodness in art and style such as beauty, drama, meaningfulness, depth and so forth. This is difficult to document, but if you look at movies, music and television since about 1950, you will see the rise of Cool as a factor in what is supposed to be attractive, from *The Wild One* to James Bond films to New Wave Music to Kate Moss to comic book movies. Some of our biggest movie-makers—Martin Scorsese, Quentin Tarantino and the Coen Brothers—are so Cool it hurts. Bubblegum transgressiveness has been the order of the day since at least Madonna, leading right up to—or down to—Katy Perry kissing other girls in public. I don't want to underestimate the good products of popular culture that have been created in the last 60 years—there are many—but I do want to point out that the criterion for what counts as good has, in a lot of cases, shifted to Coolness while more serious factors are neglected. Where are our time's *Lawrence of Arabia*, *The Godfather* and *Cabaret*?

Reason would tell you that drugs, tattoos, and

spending time with psychopathic TV protagonists are bad ideas, but in Cool people reason has been taken offline in favor of an operating system in which style is the code. Such a way of life is arrogant and neurotic, and it trivializes everything it touches. The ultimate reduction to the absurd here would have to be the hipsters' "ironic mustache." This is a fashion in which a man wears a mustache like, say, Tom Selleck's, as a parody.

Of course, the ironic mustache is just a symbol. The point is that Cool people let themselves be driven by ego satisfactions instead of getting out into the world. If you think about it, nicotine, alcohol and drugs are all ways of walling yourself up in your own head. So are style poses and irony. It takes a lot of energy to maintain a posture, and that's that much less energy left for engaging life.

The Wellsprings of Cool

The reason why Cool is tragedy rather than farce is that the quest for a distinctive style, when it isn't purely an attempt to triumph over others, can be an attempt to achieve something good. Cool is called "cool" because it entails being composed, rather than hot and reactive. Cool endeavors to be free from the control of others. Both Vanguard and Outsider Cool people think that uncool people have buttons that can easily be pushed and that such people are therefore unfree. Square people tend to be slightly hysterical, or worse, control freaks, who, of course, always feel that they are in danger of losing control.

On this view, the stylistic tics and mannerisms of Cool are a way of preserving the self in the face of society's pressure to conform. You could even regard them as misguided attempts at serenity and oneness with the cosmos. At their very best they constitute a kind of grace. I've met a few Cool people who transcended the competitive aspect of Coolness and achieved that grace, although I can't think of any famous examples except older men such as Louis Armstrong and Morgan Freeman. Unfortunately, even with these somewhat good intentions, more of the Cool still end up aggrandizing themselves than freeing themselves. This is because with Cool rejects reason, which leads to things being defined by non-essentials. Defining by non-essentials is like putting a warp in your pool table: it makes it impossible to get a clean shot. Thus it is that Cool people confuse independence from others with superiority to others.

Cool people don't want to submit to things they regard as authority, and reason is high on the list for many of them. What's Cool's objection to reason? Part of it is primalism, of course, but not all. While there are Cool intellectuals, generally speaking Coolness runs on intuition, not deliberation. Reason is held by many Cool people to be cold, unimaginative and hegemonic, meaning that it shuts out other points of view. Coolness tends to be a left-wing phenomenon, and thinkers on the intellectual left, such as the multiculturalists and the feminists, have serious doubts about the validity of reason, which they regard as a tool of domination—phallogocentrism some of them call it. In any case, Cool people want "freedom," something that makes each self a little master of the universe, mashing his own personal style onto the world. Each person being free sounds democratic and nice, but when that means, "free *of reason*," culture becomes a contest, where the winner is whoever has the bravado to impress other people into bowing before his style. Much of Cool is just cockiness, because when you take reason off the table, people with ambition will not strive for excellence and self-perfection but for status, charisma, power—the sub-rational values of primalism.

We have been very lucky so far that Cool people in America have been content to merely posture at superiority rather than strive for actual power, because the Coolest figure of the last hundred years is not James Dean but Che Guevara, the Coolest logo is not the Nike swoosh but the swastika and the biggest devotees of the Zeitgeist are not the folks at Apple but the Communists. I am not claiming that Cool people are proto-fascists or Marxists. To say so would be hysteria on my part. Most Cool people are too decent (or too lazy) to be seriously malevolent. We did have some Cool revolutionaries in the U.S. in the 1960s and 70s, but most of them couldn't liberate a loaf of bread from an oven. Germans and Italians were much better at domestic terrorism than we'll ever be—thank goodness. But even though Cool Americans are not fascists or Marxists, they have still been seduced by history's coolest president as he spies on the nation, sics the IRS on his political opponents and wiretaps the Associated Press in pursuit of the source of embarrassing leaks. The liberal media has acted like lap dogs about all this, and the protests of the right are in vain because, as everybody knows, they are a bunch of hysterical squares .

Overall I don't believe that most Cool people understand their own beliefs and practices explicitly enough to be held fully accountable for all the ramifications. Perhaps the greatest source of human tragedy is that people can believe things without identifying them explicitly or thinking through their implications. They go by what sounds good or feels good or by pseudo sense of life or ego satisfaction, rather than by actual content or consequences. One doesn't have to be a philosopher to apply a little common sense and refrain from living in a fantasy, but if one believes reason to be "uncool," one is not going to do so.

Now if we want to kill Cool, it should be obvious what we need to do: address the corruption of reason that lays the groundwork for it, kill the mystical concept of the Zeitgeist, meet and beat the quest for superiority, and address stylism —while at the same time changing some of the institutional features of society that inspire Coolness. Sounds pretty easy, doesn't it?

Exorcizing the Time-Spirit

The four essential characteristics of Cool are stylism, desire for superiority, alleged esoteric wisdom about the Zeitgeist and an excessive respect for popular culture. Each of these needs to be dismantled if we are to kill Cool.

The first aspect of Cool that must be challenged is stylism. Style has assumed in many people's minds a greater importance than reason or even morality. Without better guidance from philosophy, some people take their style to be their core identity. This is a mistake, but it is an understandable one, because style is intimately bound up with sense of life, which is near the core of the self. The real core of the self, however, is not style or sense of life but our free will, which consists of our ability to focus our attention on reality. Focusing makes the world seem present to us and makes the self more present in the world. In focus, the self achieves its full reality and can break out of its fantasies. All the other ways in which people fundamentally define themselves—style, ethnicity, a relationship to an imaginary God—are ways of avoiding the self and burrowing more deeply into their fantasies. For more on free will, see my essay on the subject, available on Kindle.

Next is the quest for superiority. A belief in one's Cool superiority is particularly difficult to abandon. What one must give up is any sense that we are special because one is ahead of the pack or apart from the pack. The quest for superiority is destructive and shallow. (To clarify, the quest for superiority to others is not the same as the quest for one's personal best, which is of course a good thing.) Being the top dog or a member of the in-group or even a member of the far-out group is ultimately not important, because one should foster one's specialness, not one's superiority, which is usually imaginary anyway. Specialness is purely an attribute of the individual in the context of her own life. We do not have to worry about being truly "special," because if we strive to perfect ourselves, we cannot help but be special, since each of us brings unique gifts, experiences and understandings to the world. That this has been said before does not make it any less true.

Esotericism must also be combated. The idea that

privileged people can tune in to the Zeitgeist is the cornerstone of Cool. With it, the Cool are justified; without it, Cool people are nothing but folks with an attitude. Needless to say, the mystical version of the Zeitgeist concept has no basis in reality. The fundamental philosophic error here is a belief in spiritual forces. The only spiritual forces in the world are those within human beings. The rest of the universe is just nature.

The biggest component of Zeitgeist thinking that needs to be attacked is the feeling of inevitability or rightness for the moment. There is no inevitability to human affairs: We are free all the way down, free enough even to violate our biological programming. Intellectually, we are only limited in that it takes time to think of something better than what we already have. We can challenge the trends of our era, and we do so by challenging our fundamental ideas.

The Zeitgeist is one of a category of externalized spiritual forces, all of which should be rejected. This category includes karma, luck, Murphy's Law—and God. I understand that most people aren't going to stop believing in God just to address the Coolness problem, but let's at least go after the concepts of Zeitgeist, karma, Murphy's Law and luck. And if you believe in God, give some thought to how the idea of an immaterial spirit reinforces those other ideas, too, because they all project intentions onto the universe where there are none. If you're a believer and you're reading this, you've probably rejected a hundred forms of superstition. I'm suggesting you reject just one more.

I will discuss the philosophy behind secularizing the world in the conclusion of this book, but I will mention here that you can go a long way toward secularization by simply accepting the fact that while emotions and other feelings have enormous heuristic value and can lead you to look in fruitful places for the truth, they are not a direct source of knowledge in the way in which the senses and logic are. People feel all sorts of things to be true, when they are not. You do it and so do I. Feelings are nothing more than how the organism registers evaluations, be they verbal or nonverbal; and our evaluations, like all of our thoughts, can be true or false—and they're much more likely to be false if we habitually put them beyond the reach of reason by miscategorizing them as instincts, faith or intuitions. The universe is not made of feelings, does not have feelings, does not respond to feelings and ultimately is not known by feelings. This means there is no valid esoteric wisdom of any type, including the instincts of the primalist, the faith of the faithful, or the intuitions of the Cool.

We must also challenge specific manifestations of the Zeitgeist concept. For example, the notion of decades, while a handy way to refer to cultural trends, can be too easily treated as a mystical concept if we let ourselves believe that those trends magically correspond to arbitrary ten-year spans. Trying to come up with a flavor for each decade ultimately pushes one toward the idea of a mystical Zeitgeist. Various important trends last more than a decade (the Civil Rights Movement), less than a decade (the presidency of John F. Kennedy), across decade boundaries (the Vietnam War). One trend can occur at the same time as a conflicting trend (the hippies and the Apollo program). To slap a label like "sixties" on all this as if there were an underlying unity to it is simply fraudulent. To be sure, there are deep underpinnings to events in the form of philosophy, science, technology and art, but they unfold as people develop them, not automatically, and they are on staggered and unpredictable timelines. Giving up on the decade idea will undoubtedly make our tidy narratives messier, but abandoning this modern numerology will also create hope, as we free ourselves from a false sense of inevitability.

The last essential characteristic of Cool that needs to be attacked is the emphasis on popular culture. This is difficult, not least of all because popular culture does have a place in a sophisticated life. It's just that popular culture is not emotionally rich enough and does not enough invite one to exercise one's powers of discernment to be one's primary spiritual nourishment.

In addition, people have the wrong idea about higher culture: They believe it consists of only classics like Shakespeare and Beethoven. Well, I believe that Shakespeare and Beethoven should be part of every educated person's life, but there is plenty of higher culture being produced today, too. I would include TV shows such as *Mad Men* and *The Wire* as high culture, as well as novels such as Donna Tartt's *The Secret History*, just to name a few examples. It's tougher for me to name a lot of modern music that I would think is high culture, because music is so much a matter of personal taste, but I might nominate, more or less at random, the album *Rabbit Songs* by the group Hem or anything by Lhasa de Sela. One could certainly argue with all of my choices, but the important thing is that one look for quality beyond Cool and that one pursue timelessness in one's tastes.

Rock and Roll High School

The next piece of the Coolness complex to be dismantled is institutional: The modern high school is a crucible for the formation of Cool. It crams volatile young people together, regiments them mercilessly and encourages the formation of cliques: jocks, cheerleaders, brains, vocational students, stoners, Christians, etc. There are adult teachers and guidance counselors among high school students, of course, but the young people are almost entirely left to their own devices socially and culturally. High school students and possibly college freshmen and sophomores are no more ready for this than eight-year olds are. Adolescents desperately need an adult presence in their lives, as a mentor, role model, stabilizing influence, etc.

Our two kinds of Cool people emerge from the bubbling cauldron of high school: the Vanguard consists of the beautiful people and the trendsetters, while the Outsiders comprise a shifting alliance of artists, high-functioning druggies, blue-collar Marlon Brando types and kids with a mouth on them, all united by their detestation of the alpha males and females and determined to find and be something more interesting than what they behold around them. Wannabes join, or try to join, these two core groups and can help them achieve a demographic critical mass. While these groups start to dissipate at commencement, the mindset often doesn't. Many people carry high school on their backs long after graduation. Sometimes this is due to trauma (as in having been bullied), sometimes it is due to not wishing to give up the advantages they felt they had there, sometimes it is due to a sheer lack of imagination. It is tough to stop Pretending, whatever the original motivation for it.

Cool people of all kinds define themselves against the flock partly because they do not want to be just another member of the flock. Not wanting to be a sheep is an understandable goal, and we should make it easier to attain. Parents are forever trying to get their children to resist peer pressure. Suggestion: Show young people that the herd isn't that important by herding them less. That means imposing as little regimentation as possible. Physical Education class, especially, should be rid of its militaristic tendencies or abolished. Whatever questionable benefits there might be to 45 minutes of unenthusiastic exercise are surely offset by the psychic cruelty it imposes. I know that large public high schools can't be run like Summerhill (a school in England that does not coerce children), but we surely could move a bit in that direction. We should start by not building such large high schools, which of necessity have to be run like cattle ranches.

Despite the veneer of rebelliousness, young people generally want to be led. Leaving them on their own creates a *Lord of the Flies* situation. The slightly older or more confident adolescents lead the younger ones. (Think of the bands, composed of 20-year-olds, that have more influence over some teenagers' lives than their parents or teachers do.)   Youth culture—hype, hormones and hot-headedness, all shaped and pandered to by the adult media and manufacturers--is one of the most destructive developments of the twentieth century. Teenagers just aren't ready to create their own culture. I am very much not saying that adolescents should be seen and not heard—they desperately need to be heard by *adults* who can help them develop their thoughts and their characters to the fullest so they can stand on their own. But young people absolutely shouldn't be left at the mercy of MTV and the wildlings of the local high school. One might as well send one's child out on an ice floe.

To counteract this tendency, I would investigate the possibility of getting mentors from the community, perhaps from the ranks of older, stable influences from the neighborhood and the business community to be part of students lives, ideally at a ratio of about ten students to one mentor. Perhaps organizations like the Scouts could help in this regard. Such measures would probably reduce the crime and teen pregnancy rates, too. If you don't want students to follow gang leaders, give them wholesome leaders, ones that will encourage them to think for themselves so that they eventually won't have to follow any leaders. But if we really want this to work, we need to kill Cool.

What Can Parents and Society Do?

Young people "catch" their culture from their parents, their peers and the media like a cold. If you want your children to ignore the "herd," you should ignore the herd yourself. Opt out of fashion. Don't buy a Coach bag. And don't try to be hip with your children. They'll just think you're lame. Find something contemplative to do with them, such as fishing or astronomy. One of my mother's greatest gifts to my siblings and me was that she read poetry with us. Such activities diffuse hype, which is the basis of most Pretending and

Cool, and help youngsters (and adults!) to engage their physical and cultural environment with something other than superficial obsessions with style.

If we want to kill Cool, we need to make its presuppositions explicit. Let's not worship Cool, humor it or pander to it. Stare Cool people right in the eye and be so confident that their attempts to be superior just collapse. Smile at them, for you know them better than they know you. But always by your manner invite them to be special rather than superior.

I would love to see a documentary that explored Cool along the lines of this essay, one that was sensitive to Cool people's desire for freedom and, in their own way, for excellence, but that also put on display their ephemeral and silly fads, the broken lives and deaths due to smoking or drugs. Getting a serious musician to explain the style of today's music in basic terms would be a wonderful way of pulling back the curtain and exposing the cultural mechanism of our time. This should all be presented in an understated way. It would be great if a film like this could be shown to teenagers. Get across that the hot things of today will be as dated in 15 years as the hot things of 15 years ago are now. Communicate that one of the keys to true greatness is to become timeless.

And if we must have public service announcements against smoking and drugs at all, let's have one with a person who has lung cancer narrating how he started smoking, showing pictures of himself when he was young and Cool. Make it intimate and don't try to outcool Cool—that just reinforces the concept. (The "this is your brain on drugs" ads were more hilarious than anything else.) Make the message so heartfelt and compelling and non-pedantic that it can't be satirized. It's difficult to get this message across, not just because kids think they're invulnerable, but because kids think they have an all-powerful ally in the mystical Zeitgeist, which is why that concept must be exposed, mocked and destroyed.

Lastly, we should start finding ways of portraying alternatives to Cool for young people to buy into to: models of ways of life that are adventurous, non-reactive, reasonable, independent and focused on doing something interesting with one's time in the world. I'm not fond of fantasy stories (See "The Vampire and the Last Man") but I suppose Harry Potter might help in this regard with kids of a certain age. But rather than feeding kids more stories, it might be better to hook them at an early age on exploratory or creative activities such as photography or being a maker or naturalism or collecting oral histories from older relatives and neighbors. But this healthy vision should be as little institutionalized as possible; the primary motivation should come from within the young person, and adult suggestions should be tentative and without pressure. If all this is going to work, however, it will be necessary to get the young person away from the TV, the computer, the iPod, the phone, the sugar and the caffeine. Help them become grounded. Hype creates a kind of feverish state that makes it much easier to be dazzled by visions of the Zeitgeist.

Concluding Unscientific Postscript

Killing Cool is the right thing to do. Cool is a form

of Pretending that is based on a false concept, namely the mystical Zeitgeist. When we define ourselves with reference to a false concept, we necessarily falsify the self. How much cleaner and more authentic life would be if we were to abandon this clammy illusion! But to make a change in our lives, we have to make a change in our thoughts, because our current way of thinking isn't doing the job, isn't saving the quarter of a million lives each year, isn't making sure all that potential doesn't go to waste.

A person who is not Cool is a person who is free to be herself. She is free from the pressure to compete with anyone and to keep up with the mystical, mythical Zeitgeist. She doesn't have to hide behind fashionable shades and fashionable shoes. She will smile more than a Cool person does. She won't be posing and so she will be free to explore the world more and get to know other people on their own terms instead of as potential conquests or co-conspirators. She won't smoke or abuse alcohol or drugs. She will be summer to Cool's winter.

Notice that my prescription for changing damaging behavior by killing Cool is not about trying to propagandize young people. That would be a mistake. We should always start by taking an ecological approach, using the natural processes within the system and looking at our part in creating the problem. People don't naturally want to be Cool, and they're much less likely to try to be Cool if what Cool is about is brought out into the open. We need to de-mystify Cool, starting with our own attempts to be Cool.

What this means is if we want to kill Cool in others, we must first kill the concept of Zeitgeist in our own lives and stop defining ourselves in terms of our alleged superiority to others. First and foremost it is about changing ourselves, changing the values of society at large—your values and mine—so as to deflate the cultural hype and heavy-handed institutions in which we live, environments that create a niche in which Cool can flourish.

Demon Rum

Here's a question for you: What's the fastest way to get someone to reach for a drink? Answer: Tell him he shouldn't drink. According to Claude Steiner, author of *Games Alcoholics Play*, serious drinking always contains an element of the rebellious child proclaiming, "I'm drunk and I'm proud!"

Well, if you're looking for an excuse to drink, don't look to me. I'm not going to tell you not to drink. If you're reading this, you're a grown-up, and you can make your own decisions. Instead, I'm going to tell you why *I* don't drink (and by implication why I don't use drugs). If you think my reasons apply to you, then apply them.

One reason I don't drink is alcoholism. It runs in my family. I estimate that if I were to drink more than a single drink once in a while (which is all I ever did), my chances of becoming an alcoholic would be about 50%. That's like Russian Roulette with three bullets in the gun. And I know what some of my relatives were like when they were drunk. They were cruel, they acted like idiots, they passed out in public, and they wrecked their marriages. My father, who was an alcoholic, nearly cracked my skull open once by knocking me down when I was 10 years old. Of course, I don't have to tell you about how badly people behave when they're drunk. Besides, you're in no danger of becoming an alcoholic, are you?

Being around my alcoholic father made me decide when I was eight years old that I would never get drunk, and I never have. I also decided not to smoke. Decisions like this helped me to form solid ego boundaries and to take responsibility for myself. Having a firm identity has made it easier for me to be independent. Peer pressure passed right through me, because it couldn't touch what I was. People who drink and smoke and have sex because of peer pressure mold themselves to others' desires. They are chips in the flood, rather than rocks in the stream. They can't stand up to the pressure because they aren't anything definite.

Now you might be thinking I must be a fundamentalist or a prig. I assure you that I'm not. I can't be a fundamentalist because I have never believed in God. I don't base my non-drinking on authority, be it God's or society's, nor on some abstract notion of duty. My reason for not drinking isn't that I think I'm not "supposed to" drink. I don't drink because it doesn't make sense to me. As for being a prig, well, I'm not a very good candidate for that title because prigs posture as being better than other people, and I'm far too self-centered to compare myself to other people.

Drinkers often use fantasy images about non-drinkers, such as fundamentalist or prig, to shore up their drinking habit, which almost all serious drinkers feel slightly guilty about. Many drinkers compensate by trying to tell themselves that non-drinkers are moralizers or that they are naïve about grown-up pleasures or whatnot. In case you haven't figured it out, what I am doing here is closing off your escape routes. I'm not going to tell you not to drink, because that's up to you, but I'm not going to let you dismiss my reasons for not drinking on account of what you might falsely imagine about my character.

So, other than the practical reason of not wanting to become an alcoholic, why don't I drink? What if there were a genetic test for alcoholism and I could be certain that I couldn't become an alcoholic—would I drink then?

No.

First of all, and nobody can argue with this point, I just don't like how drinking alcohol feels. One drink makes me queasy, flushed, slightly disoriented. It's kind of like having the flu. Obviously the experience of drinking is not so unpleasant for most drinkers, or they wouldn't drink.

Actually, I'm not so sure about that. It's well known that our expectations about experiences can color our underlying perceptions even to the point of reversing them. When Hamlet says "There is nothing either good or bad, but thinking makes it so," he is overstating the case, but there is a large grain of truth in his words. Let me explain with an example: When I was 25, I ruptured a disc in my lower back and was immobilized and in screaming pain (yes, I actually screamed). The doctor put me on Percocet (a narcotic) and Robaxin (a muscle relaxer). I was very relieved to be out of (most of the) pain and I lay in bed watching beautiful spirals of light forming tunnels before me. I was pretty happy. But then I thought about it. What did I have to be happy about? I couldn't even get out of bed without help. Every four hours the medicine wore off and I was in pain again. I couldn't even go to the bathroom by myself.

When I put it that way to myself, I no longer felt happy. I just felt as if I had had an idiot grin pasted on my face. When I examined what I actually felt physically, I saw that it was mostly a lack of pain, a muffling of sensation, and a kind of steady, low pleasure that was actually slightly annoying, because it was unconnected to anything in my life. It was like getting a massage when I didn't want to get a massage. The euphoria I had felt before came from my expectation that the Percocet would give me narcotic pleasure, plus my elation at not being in screaming pain any more.

I know at this point that some readers are thinking, "Congratulations, Bozo, you spoiled a really good high, one for which you had a Get Out of Jail card, since you needed the medication."

True. But I do not see it as spoiling. Feeling happy without a cause is, in my opinion, not true happiness. If it's not real, it's not worth it. I'll come back to this point later.

On the subject of coloring perceptions, I have sometimes wondered what would be the outcome of two experiments on people, one in which you convinced subjects that they were drinking alcohol when they were not, and one where you convinced subjects they were not drinking alcohol when they were. It turns out such experiments have been done, and you can read about them at http://www.morerevealed.com/mr/

drinking.html. The result: people who believed they had drunk alcohol acted in a more uninhibited manner than people who didn't believe they had, whether they actually had or not.

I am just speculating, since the report didn't comment on this matter, but I would guess that the people who had been given alcohol when they believed that they had not been would *not* get the typical euphoria, but would merely feel bare physical sensations just as I did on Percocet after I thought about it. Perhaps they would feel they were coming down with the flu as I felt when I used to drink a little. Or maybe they might not notice at all, although their system would be depressed, their reaction time slowed, their sexual response made more sluggish, etc.

(Another experiment discussed on the same webpage found that heroin users could be hypnotized into thinking they had gotten a fix, even to the point of their eyes dilating. The placebo effect is a powerful thing and is strong evidence for mind-body integration.)

I would draw two tentative conclusions from these experiments: First, the joy of drinking probably depends largely upon the culture of drinking. This culture consists of expectations of lowered inhibitions, rituals like toasts, infantile pet names for booze ("brewskis," "martoonies"), a celebratory desire to destroy rational functioning (get wasted, smashed, hammered, shit-faced, etc.), and so on, all wrapped in the high-class, low-class connoisseurship of single-malt whiskey and micro-brew beer. The pleasure of drinking lies mostly, I hypothesize, in participating in this culture and its various pseudo senses of life. Serious drinking is like being Cool: it is anti-reason, it involves esoteric wisdom (allegedly obtained through alcohol), it seeks superiority over non-drinkers, and it values the artificial inner experience over the wonders of the real world. Drinking differs from Cool in that drinking substitutes an alcoholic élan for the stylism of Cool. This quasi-Cool culture of drinking is the point for the serious drinker. The alcohol is just there to make it a little more convincing. That's why drinking alone just isn't as much fun; people need others around them to help sustain the illusion.

My second conclusion is the flipside of the first: People can have the joy of drinking without the actual alcohol. That is not to say that I myself am interested in *exactly* the kind of pleasure that drinkers have. People who are drunk do boring and stupid things and can be unpleasant to be around, unless you are also drunk. But a less unappealing but still carefree, loose and fun-loving state of mind is also possible without the alcohol. Perhaps we can adjust our mood without liquid support.

My own experience confirms this. I remember the summer after my senior year of high school. A lot of my classmates were drinking during that period, but my friends and I didn't. We still had incredible fun. We would joke until one of us literally fell on the floor laughing. We would go to the midnight movies. A couple of times we sneaked under the gate to Oak Ridge Cemetery and hung out on Abraham Lincoln's tomb, sitting in the dark listening to spooky sounds off in the distance. And of course there was making out at the drive-in. Would these experiences have been improved by alcohol? We were plenty uninhibited and playful without it.

Of course, injured people need pain meds and mentally ill people need psych meds. I am definitely not saying that hypnosis and a good attitude are a cure for all our ills. I am telling you why I don't drink: I don't drink because I don't want pleasure forced down my throat, as it were, and because I know how to get a natural high.

Please don't get the idea that I am holding myself up as an ideal role model. I'm not. I have enough problems for two people. But there are some things I do get right. For example, I try to be oriented toward reality. If something's not real, then it can't have any value. For example, a marriage where one partner has evidence that the other is cheating is not a good marriage, and living in denial does not make it better. Of course, drinking isn't the only way to make the unreal seem real, but dwelling in fantasy is easier if you fill your tank with ethanol. The serious drinker believes that feelings are as good as facts, which suggests he doesn't fully know the difference.

For years I have struggled mightily to get out of my own head and into the world. The crisp feeling of living in reality is a thing of beauty: it's like a gentle breeze that makes you aware of both the air and your own skin. Drinking alcohol or using drugs, however, would be a step in the wrong direction. In fact, I suspect that getting drunk or high requires that one already live in one's head, out of any real context. But since I don't drink, I don't have a definite opinion on this subject, and I'm not trying to tell anybody what his or her experience is. It would be true for me, however.

People are usually trying to achieve some partial good by drinking. In fact, people aim at something good in most of the things they do, even the unwise things. The point of philosophy and psychology as I understand them is to help people clarify and untangle what they are trying to achieve and find the best means to the end. I have no problem with people wanting to unwind or have fun or be silly or get sexy. I am sober in the sense that I don't drink, but I am not sober in the sense of always being serious and somber. I just understand fun somewhat differently from most serious drinkers.

One big example of fun for me these days is to go exploring new places with my wife, either on foot or on bike. There's nothing like getting out in the world and seeing its limitless splendor. On one biking trip two years ago we found a beautiful grotto hidden by the side of the trail, a five-hundred-square-foot mural of a picturesque old railroad station, and the best pizza we ever had outside of New Haven. Add to this the wonder of flying through nature on our bikes and what you have is joy. Compare this to the pleasure, if such it be, of hanging out in a musty bar, with a lot of people making fools of themselves and a bathroom that smells like vomit. As far as I am concerned, there isn't room in the same universe for both experiences.

Maybe one reason why people feel they need alcohol is that they are stuck in what they perceive to be the Rational Adult mode of functioning. They feel they have to be controlled and responsible and serious and unemotional (except for the emotion of worry). For them the equation is: alcohol + the expectations that come with it = a way out. Alcohol gives them a switch with which they can turn the Rational Adult off.

This of course presupposes that reason is opposed

to emotion and spontaneity. It doesn't have to be. Mr. Spock was wrong about this. However, if you habitually think about your values, you can trust your emotional expressions. And spontaneity is compatible with reason, as long as your reason first decides that you're in a safe environment to be spontaneous in. Then you can just play.

As a writer who does a lot of thinking, I very much do not oppose my feelings and my reason. For me, thinking consists of taking my reactions to the world seriously, testing them and fleshing them out. Look at the process of discovery I described in "The Pretender." It took me a long time, but by exploring my impressions, I was able to arrive at a useful concept. I try to do something similar in my personal life, too.

"Exploration" is the key metaphor of my life, ironically for a man who has never even been to Canada. That doesn't stop me: "I could be bounded in a nutshell and count myself a king of infinite space." I believe in free will and I think that our basic choice consists of whether or not to explore the world cognitively. My favorite recreation, and indeed my vocation, is discovering the wonders of the world. Drinking would be like being stuck in the same old place, feeling the same old feelings, telling the same old jokes.

I don't talk much in this book about art appreciation, but it is an area where I think most serious drinkers are deprived. Of course, the wine connoisseur who is also an art connoisseur is a cliché, but a much more common phenomenon is the person who drinks so that the world will look beautiful/friendly/interesting to him. I can relate to this. When I was young I felt starved for meaning and for beauty. I knew that my adolescent love of *Dune* and The Who would not sustain me into adulthood. My natural hunger for values led me over the decades to build up a collection of photography, music, movies and literature that I think is exquisite. I didn't plan to do this. I didn't pursue culture as a chore or because an educated person is "supposed to" like Shakespeare and Beethoven and landscapes— no, I just followed my taste and challenged my taste and in the process developed my taste. But this process would have been subverted if I had been willing to content myself with the "beauty" of *American Pie 2* as viewed through the bottom of a beer bottle. Alcohol lubricates the process of settling for less.

The experiments with making people think that they had drunk alcohol or taken heroin when they hadn't suggest that in some situations at least, you can affect your feelings toward life with a good attitude. I try to achieve a positive outlook by adopting a constructive stance or by looking for beauty—and, as necessary, by examining the beliefs that hold me back. I don't paste a contrived sense of life over reality; my ingenuous and ingenious sense of life consists of seeing in the world opportunities for achievement and wonder and engagement. I started developing this view as a child by exploring the world and its possibilities, both by bike and by book. I didn't grab my worldview off the rack as a Pretender would.

My sense of life is tailored to me. Not everyone is looking for what I am looking for in life. Nor should they be. For example, I am big on earnestness. Other people who are more self-sufficient than I am and have a faster metabolism than I do might gravitate toward what's bracing in life and engage in more banter than I do, and that's OK. Sense of life is one of those things that can legitimately vary—with temperament and natural abilities, with experience and family of origin, with what's available to you in nature and your culture. Being rational does not require that we all be the same. The important thing is to search for values in the world and not just give in to inertia or insecurities. In the process you'll grow an unforced set of feelings about the basic opportunities the world affords you—and that's what a real sense of life is.

Life to me is transcendently beautiful, like walking into a cathedral, and life to me is an adventure, like charging down a wooded hill on my bike. I am not imposing this view on reality as a Pretender would; I discovered it about the world as it relates to me. I reconnect with my sense of life feelings many times a day. The subway stations I wait in during my commute, with their vaulted ceilings, are my cathedrals. The thunder of the trains approaching is like Beethoven. I feel that my writing illuminates the architecture of the world. My wife is the most beautiful woman I have ever seen. *What do I need alcohol for?*

You may not share my appreciation of subway trains. Fine. Different people find different things exciting, of course. I'm not at all trying to say everyone should be like me. But surely there are better things in almost everyone's life than sitting around in a bar or on the couch in front of a football game getting drunk. But you have to find those things yourself. I can't tell you what they are for you, which is why I'm not entitled to tell you not to drink. But I can tell you that the world is inexhaustible in what it offers, and if you're not seeing something better than alcohol, you're not looking hard enough.

To sum up, I don't drink because I am concerned about alcoholism, because I don't like the effect and because I don't have the expectations that would make the effect seem pleasurable, because I think things are only valuable when they're real, and because I can get the benefits of drinking without the actual intoxication. I used to drink a little before the foregoing gelled for me. Then I stopped, and I don't miss it.

Drinking just isn't part of the good life, as far as I am concerned. It's up to you whether or not you will drink, and while the occasional glass of wine or beer is no doubt harmless, I think my reasons for not drinking are worth considering. I am not saying that the good life always comes easily to me. Sometimes I really have to work at it. But through it all I always I return to the real world with all of its splendor, and that refreshes me as no beverage ever could.

Faith and the Bubble Universe

Cards on the table: I am an atheist. I have never believed in God. And I am not some wishy-washy agnostic who "doesn't know" whether God exists or not. I know: the traditional concept of God is a self-contradictory impossibility with no evidentiary support. People who believe in God may be decent and worthwhile human beings, but they are making a serious mistake. Furthermore, my opinion of religion is very low. For example, the concept of Hell, which several religions share, is simply hateful, unjust and barbaric.

I am not here to debate religion with the reader. Every argument for the existence of God has been reduced to rubble a hundred times over. You can easily check this out if you want to. The very fact that believers have to make arguments for the existence of something as supposedly omnipresent as God is itself a demonstration that we need not take the idea of God seriously. You don't have to make arguments for the existence of the sun. Instead of providing yet another set of arguments against the existence of God, I would like to analyze the practice of faith that sustains Christianity and to offer tentative suggestions for how to talk with Christian believers, if you want to reach out to them. In this discussion I am going to confine myself to Christianity, because although much of my analysis could be applied to other religions, I really don't know enough about them to comment on them in detail.

Onward, Atheist Soldiers!

It's wonderful that some atheists are willing to carry the banner into battle by engaging in debate with Christians. But in my opinion straightforward arguments will only win a few people over to our side. There are psychological reasons for this failure that I think we need to understand if we atheists are to have a meaningful dialogue with believers. I think an approach may emerge from examining these reasons that will make it more likely that atheists will help (some) believers to give up their mistaken worldview.

The project of ridding society of Christian influence is made more difficult by the existence of people who want it both ways. Some atheists, for example, believe in keeping Christian morality while chucking God. The "secular humanist" camp largely believes in the service-to-society ideal of Christianity. Sometimes I wonder whether they aren't closet Unitarians. Nietzsche, whom I enjoy quoting even though he's wrong about most things, correctly said that if you get rid of the Christian God, you are not entitled to Christian ethics, which very much do not stand on their own. Religious ideas about being one's "brother's keeper" are neither true nor healthy; Christian ethics are just as wrong as the rest of the religion. The secular humanists, to the extent they advocate service to society, just muddy the water.

And just as some atheists try to retain Christian values, some Christians seek to appropriate the values of the Enlightenment, a time of reason and worldliness, if not outright atheism. They claim that American society is primarily built on religious ethics, when in fact it was based on Enlightenment values of commonsense, tolerance, self-reliance and happiness through productiveness. It superficially looks as if religion built America because religion watered itself down and allied itself with Enlightenment values, creating a uniquely American cocktail. But the main ingredient is reason, not faith.

Christians and atheists have a "failure to communicate." I know this from personal experience. Most recently, I've had a couple of discussions on Facebook with a serious Christian whom I've never actually met. They didn't go well. I didn't make arguments to him, since I thought these were futile, so I mostly tried to undermine his point of view with clever remarks. We'll write that off as a learning experience.

Now I would like to try to figure out a better approach so that if this issue comes up again, I'll know what to do. Perhaps other atheists could experiment with these ideas and we could develop an effective method. To do this we need to have a look at the nature of mistakes in general, since after all Christianity in all its forms is a kind of mistake.

The Nature of Error, or How to Make a Mistake

Everybody makes mistakes. Everybody sometimes believes things that are not true. Human beings are fallible and should not judge themselves harshly when they make an honest error. Our own mistakes and the mistakes of other people are of concern to us, because we want to know how to make fewer of them, and because we want to know whether they are honest or not. And while we should of course work on our own possible mistakes first, we want to know how to help others put their errors right, without being moralistic or condescending.

Not all mistakes are created equal. My belief that we have enough butter to last until the weekend and someone's belief that they might realistically win the lottery are not the same kind of error. We need to understand the difference.

There are two somewhat overlapping sources of error in human life. One comes from faulty processing. Mistakes here range from optical illusions, to limited memory, to being in a hurry, to various passive cognitive biases. Such errors are easily correctable with further evidence, and people usually don't stubbornly hold on to them, unless pride gets in the way. These errors are involuntary since one was not trying to see the situation in a false way.

Other errors involve a voluntary component. The wishful thinking that makes people throw money away on the lottery is voluntary. That's not to say people fully understand what they're doing when they do it. Voluntary errors are possible because we can do things without identifying them explicitly. As Molière points out, we can speak prose without knowing it. A voluntary error is perpetrated consciously, but not with full, explicit awareness of what is being done. (For example, all Pretending is voluntary error.) This claim that we can do things without having an explicit identification of them is one of the most important principles for the reasonable application of moral standards, because it mitigates many deeds that would be morally repugnant if they were committed with full consciousness.

A fundamental difference between an involuntary error and a voluntary one is that an involuntary error is not motivated and a voluntary one is. If I thought I saw four cans of soup on the shelf instead of three because I was in a hurry, it's not that I desperately wanted there to be four cans of soup. On the other hand, if I kid myself that my cube-mate is attracted to me because I am attracted to her, that is probably a motivated error. I was at some level trying to see things that way. Still, if I am not aware of the thought process I engaged in, it is not necessarily an evasion of truth.

Evasion of the truth is the hallmark of immorality. If there is an action we know to be wrong and we perform it anyway, then must be something in the nature of the situation or the quality of the action that we are evading or we would not perform it. But if we do not know that the action is wrong, we are morally blameless. At most we are guilty of poor cognitive hygiene, which might betoken a character flaw, or we might just be the victims of bad education. In any case, if "they know not what they do," they should be forgiven.

Some voluntary errors do involve an outright evasion of what is known, sacrificing the truth to some emotional goal. The outright evasion makes the error immoral. The anti-Semitism of the Nazis would be an example of this. Many Germans seemed to feel a generalized resentment, partly because of their own twisted philosophy and partly because they felt humiliated in losing WWI. Anti-Semitism gave their resentments a concrete object, a whipping boy. Such people prop up their false beliefs by pseudo-science and the group mind. They could not readily give up their prejudices about Jews, because to do so would have meant confronting their deepest convictions and their feelings of humiliation. Most of them would probably rather have died than do so.

That Jews are human beings is patently obvious. For the Nazis to believe what they believed and to have done what they did required a massive evasion of a fact that stared them in the face. Furthermore, it took a willingness to suppress (i.e. evade) their own basic loving nature as human beings in order to unleash such vehement and destructive hatred. It may seem incredible to say that Nazis had a loving nature, but everyone who does not have a mental disorder such as psychopathy does at some level. Even Hitler had some love in him—look at his affection for dogs. Yet he denied that side of himself when it came to "inferior" beings, such as Jews. Denying his loving nature and denying the obvious fact that Jews are human beings are what made Hitler, as well as the other Nazis, evil. Their philosophy and its attendant pseudo sense of life represented ego satisfactions on a colossal scale and of course were voluntary errors.

Most voluntary errors are not wicked and evasive, however, but are innocent blindness or self-deception. People do sometimes face them and give them up, although with some difficulty, since trying to examine a deeply held voluntary error is like stepping on the gas and the brake at the same time. Which brings me to my main subject: How can religious people be helped to overcome their errors? Can Christians be saved?

Religious error can be of any kind. It might be involuntary if the believer has had a hallucination or a near-death event or some other experience that could reasonably, although mistakenly, be interpreted as evidence for the existence of God or an afterlife. Also, those people who are taken in by Christian apologetics may be committing an involuntary error. But most Christians maintain their beliefs by that form of wishful thinking known as faith. Faith is the choice to believe something without conclusive rational evidence, and faith is the paradigm of voluntary errors.

At this point an old Christian argument rears its head. "Don't we all believe things by faith? Your belief that George Washington was the first president of the United States is based on 'faith,' isn't it? Most of our knowledge is based on 'faith' in our teachers and schoolbooks and common opinion."

It's true that many such beliefs are not based on direct knowledge. The difference, however, is that on most of these subjects I could go and check out the truth of the matter for myself. I could go down to the National Archives and look at records that would show me that George Washington was indeed the first president of the United States. There would also be secondary evidence in terms of books and paintings and the like, of the kind that would only be created to commemorate a president and founder. There's no reason why anyone would want to make up something like that. My belief in Washington's presidency is indirect knowledge because I wasn't there, but it isn't faith, because there is evidence for it and because I have no vested interest in believing it. The Christian could suggest that for all I know the evidence was all created just a few years ago to fool people like me, but that would be to invoke the arbitrary as an authority, and no one is under any obligation to acknowledge arbitrary assertions. That principle is, by the way, why I am an atheist and not an agnostic: I know that I don't have to take seriously every idea that comes out of somebody's mouth; I don't have to think, "Well you believe it, so it *might* be true. I don't know."

True faith, religious faith, is different from the kind of indirect knowledge I have of Washington's presidency. Even though its subject (God) is much more important, no one goes and checks on it, because they can't. And people are highly motivated to believe in it even though it is not true, because they are afraid of dying or they are afraid that the universe would be meaningless without a God, etc. This motivation makes the belief suspect.

The Big Tent of Faith

Religious faith isn't wishful thinking about just one subject, such as the lottery, but about a whole worldview. In "The Pretender," I describe a person who artificially maintains a sense of life by pretending it. Such a person lives in a "Bubble Universe" because everything is filtered through the lens of his pseudo sense of life. His emotional narrative comes between him and the real world and keeps him from seeing reality and other people as they are, instead recasting them as characters in his own private drama. This is a grave problem for the Pretender, because it undermines both his objectivity and his empathy.

The seriously religious present a variation on the Pretender phenomenon because they live in a Bubble Universe, too, but one far more serious than that of the ordinary Pretender. Instead of filtering things just through a sense of life, they erect a complete "alternate reality." Instead of having the world be merely colored by sunglasses as it is for the Pretender, a belief system is interposed between the believer and the world like a wall.

Maybe I can make my claims clearer with an analogy. Faith is like a big tent that the believer puts up. The tent blocks out most of his view of the world except for peeks through the openings. The tent is held up by poles, which are the believer's motivations for his faith. The sun casts shadows of things outside the tent onto the canvas and they can be seen as silhouettes from the inside. The effect is like watching a cartoon. (Some readers will notice that this is a variation of Plato's parable of the cave.)

Now religious people don't block out reality to such an extent that they walk in front of cars, of course, but the conceptual underpinnings of their world are seriously compromised. Conservative Christians, for example, have a Bubble Universe full of rigidly held, discrete ideas, like original sin and the need for salvation by grace. I would like to examine two conservative Christian beliefs to illustrate the tent analogy. I'm not interested in quaint notions such as the virgin birth or the trinity, but in beliefs that affect how the Christian judges the real world.

The first is the belief that everything happens for a reason. Under this belief, some conservative Christians did not view Hurricane Katrina as a natural disaster that happened for purely meteorological reasons but as punishment for the sinful nature of New Orleans. The logic of this assertion is instructive. Very serious believers hold that God controls natural processes directly. If a storm wipes out a city, it's because God sent that storm.

Now if a city gets wiped out, you would expect that a lot of innocent people would die. But God sent the storm, so that means that God killed a lot of innocent people. This is not an acceptable idea to those who believe in a loving God. We can't let God be seen as brutal and malicious. The obvious way to address this situation is to say that the people killed deserved to die, because they were depraved. That lets God off the hook because now he's not killing innocent people. Of course, not even Pat Robertson would say that every man, woman and child who died in New Orleans was depraved (beyond the ordinary level of original sin). But the deaths of the innocent can be laid at the feet of their sodomizing, carousing, idolatrous neighbors, who brought down the wrath of God on the whole city. Therefore, God is exonerated: the sinful are responsible for the suffering of the (relatively) innocent!

Notice that this concern for God's reputation papers over any concern for the real-world sufferers. The conservative Christian who believes in this sort of thing has an amazing lack of empathy. I doubt that he even gives ten seconds thought to the innocent: He just thinks "New Orleans = City of Sin." The real event gets simplified to a few, largely imaginary components that are related to each other not by the logic of evidence but by the logic of the story being told. Again, it's all rather like a cartoon, where anything is possible if the big cartoonist in the sky draws it that way. The narrative, which is largely a product of the conservative's internal needs, substitutes for 90% of the reality. (The other 10% is the few shadowy facts that penetrate the believer's tent.)

The belief that everything happens for a reason means that there is no insentient but lawful nature at the foundation of the universe. Consciousness pervades every event, and the bad things that happen to you, be they hurricanes or cancer, are either your own fault or is part of an incomprehensible "plan" that one has to accept without question. The net effect is to create in human beings feelings of helplessness and guilt, which would keep one dependent on the idea of God, at least until one has had enough and breaks free.

Let's apply the tent analogy to another case: the infallibility of the Bible. Take the case of the Old Testament strictures against two men lying together. Here the tent of faith hides the reality of gay people from the believer. All he can see is the "yuckiness" of two men touching and the oft-repeated canard that straight marriage is being undermined by gay people. That's the cartoon silhouette. What doesn't cast a recognizable shadow is the honest love gay people feel for each other; the futility, proven again and again, of trying to change someone's sexual orientation; and the horrible persecution many gay people suffer, especially as teenagers. The reality of gay life is just not on the radar because the tent blocks it out.

The reliance on Old Testament laws against men lying with men is a blatant rationalization, since the Old Testament has all sorts of rules and prohibitions that modern Christians ignore, since Jesus allegedly released us from them. This is typical of how conservative Christians interpret their holy book. They cherry-pick the parts that support their views and ignore the rest, because they have so little concern for reality, not even for the reality of their Bible, except insofar as they can maintain their illusions with it. Look at the way in which many Christians torture the Old Testament to extort prophecies of Jesus' coming as the "messiah." The Jews do not consider the messiah to be God-become-man at all, but just a human king, like David—are they wrong about their own scriptures? Once again Christians blot out reality and interpret the world in accord with the dream logic of their belief system. The Bible is infallible—when it agrees with the Christian's beliefs. The rest of the time it is just ignored.

Are Christians Evil?

The religious Bubble Universe is more pervasive than regular wishful thinking, because wishful thinking usually pertains to just one facet of the world: When I play the lottery, I want to believe I will hit the jackpot; a woman whose husband is cheating wants to believe he is faithful her despite the many little hints that he is not, etc. Despite the blindness or self-deception in these cases, the wishful thinker can usually see most of life clearly. Religious faith, on the other hand, is more nearly global. Its parts are mutually reinforcing. It blocks out enough reality that it's very difficult to see how *any* evidence that would undermine its beliefs could ever get through. It is a system, an alternate reality superimposed on actual reality. The Bubble Universe is not just anchored in ego satisfactions; it is an attempt to shore up an entire, desperate worldview.

Despite all of this, I would say that religion, though a voluntary error, is still usually an honest error. I base this on the fact, which I mentioned before, that one can do something voluntarily without doing it explicitly and self-consciously. This is especially true if one started distorting one's cognition as a child before one has learned to identify one's mental functions. I don't think most American Christians know better than to believe what they believe. It seems to me they are little more than children when it comes to understanding some aspects of how the world works, especially their own minds. They have not fully separated their own minds from the world, and so they feel that the world is filled with spirit, like their lungs are filled with air. If facts are the firm boundaries that keep us from believing whatever we want, then religious folk live in a world without boundaries, only with God's intentions and to a lesser extent, ours. This is the same kind of Primacy of Consciousness error we saw in the Pollyanna Pretender earlier in the book.

There is a natural tendency for humans to project their feelings onto the world. Animals do so automatically. A cat looks at his traditional enemy, the broom. He does not say to himself, "I feel fear but I could master it." He just feels that the broom is *scary*. The emotion is attached to the object, not the subject. Humans do the same thing as children. Before they can attain emotional maturity, they have to learn, first, that the locus of an emotion is actually within the self, not the world, and second, that an emotion can be critically examined by checking the underlying thought. Religious believers have not learned these steps, at least not when it comes to their spiritual emotions. This may be a case of arrested development, but it's usually not evasion.

An error becomes an outright evasion, and therefore immoral, when it is something one could and should know better than to believe. It's very difficult to judge when someone should know better than to believe something. It involves a complicated relationship between the "size" of the error and the cognitive abilities and context of the person making it. In general I would err on the side of judging mistakes as innocent, at least until I saw evasiveness in the believer's manner. Where I would tend to summarily judge a believer immoral is where I saw that he was motivated by hatred or sadism, as some televangelists seem to be about natural disasters. Since every civilized person knows that cruelty is wrong, it requires an evasion to enjoy others' suffering.

People who actually revel in the suffering of Katrina's victims, or who feel no sympathy for gay teenagers who are bullied, are wicked. People who state "God hates fags" are wicked, because they are gloating over the suffering they imagine others feel in response to their nasty little opinions. But people *can* believe Katrina was punishment and that homosexuality goes against God's law without being malicious, if they take no pleasure in these claims. They would be seriously benighted, but they might not be immoral.

By the way, religion is not the only Bubble Universe in the realm of ideas. Psychoanalysis is a Bubble Universe. Marxism is a Bubble Universe. Even true ideas can be the basis of a Bubble Universe if you caricature them and treat them rationalistically. An example of this would be the way some evolutionists try to reduce all of human action to reproductive strategies. One can even take a true idea and switch in and out of Bubble Universe mode with it, as when one adopts or abandons a didactic, pedantic or fanatic attitude toward it. Adopting such an attitude, one gets caught up in the rightness of one's cause and intent on winning abstract arguments instead of being centered and seeing the person in front of one. Unfortunately, some atheists seem to adopt a Bubble Universe mind set when they debate believers.

How to Burst a Bubble

So what should one do when confronted with someone who lives in a religious Bubble Universe? Some religious belief is involuntary, the result of not having thought through the traditional Christian arguments (design, first cause, etc.). Such belief can be addressed through normal discussion. But most religious belief is, in my experience, voluntary. For such believers, facts and logic aren't the point, so offering facts and logic to them won't do much good. So, does that make it futile to discuss religion with such a Christian? Not exactly. We're forgetting about the poles holding up the tent. These are the motivations for sustaining the Bubble Universe. Remember that voluntary error is motivated error. I think it would be more fruitful to focus on the motivations and to try to open up the believer's access to the real world.

Now, there isn't just one motivation for believing in Christianity, not even within a single person. An individual believer might have a half dozen or so. Some of the common motivations, I think, are fear of death, fear of meaninglessness, fear that things one's authority figures have told one are false, fear of being out of control, fear that one will succumb to evil, fear of going it alone, fear of an earthly power against which one needs a more powerful ally and fear of being unloved. I'm no doubt omitting some.

Notice that the common element is fear. I think a few, very spiritual Christians are not motivated by fear but by a positive vision of a universe where everything is connected and everything is love. Such people are rare and wonderful in a way, but they are still quite fuzzy in their thinking, almost willfully blind, like the title character in the play and film *Agnes of God*. I don't enjoy saying that such people are deluded because one of the most beautiful people I have ever known was a spiritual Christian of this type. But such people, even if they are not motivated by fear, tend to have a highly selective view of the world and resist logic in any area where they have strong feelings.

Given that most Christians are motivated by fear, you can see that assailing them with arguments is counterproductive. It will only make them more frightened and defensive and increase their motives for false belief. Arguments, when made to hostile listeners, tend to be confrontational. We "attack" or "defend" a "position," etc., using military metaphors. While I do think there is a place for confrontational tactics—in debate before an audience or when calling an individual to account for a belief that is cruel, for example—in general, it is probably better to figure out what fear(s) the Christian feels and to address it. I would like to suggest the following strategies for discussing religion with a Christian. However, I should say that the occasion has not arisen for me to try these, since I do not go around looking for Christians to convert, so please take these ideas as mere suggestions from the sidelines:

1. Take a real interest in the person you're talking with and look upon your discussion as a conversation, not a debate. If you're just looking to score points, you are using another human being, and that is wrong.

2. Ask non-confrontational questions and do not make pronouncements. Good questions leave an empty space that your interlocutor is invited to fill. Don't try to back the person into a corner.

3. Focus on feelings and the impressions of life and the world that support those feelings, rather than on "official" beliefs, which are usually aspects of the Bubble Universe. When asked about your opinions, focus on *your* feelings and impressions. Think of how a natural atheist child views the world and communicate that—by example, not by lecturing.

The Christians call giving an account of their conversion "testifying." You can do the same as an atheist.

4. Ask, "What does God do for you emotionally?" not, "What reason do you have for believing in God?" Alternatively, you can ask how the Christian felt before he or she was a Christian. The answer to first question will probably be "Safe" or "Loved" or "As if my life has meaning," while the second will elicit the opposite. Whatever the answer is, follow up on it. Ask, "What is that like?" When the person is ready, which could take hours, ask: "How did the world make you feel unsafe/unloved/meaningless?" Be careful not to play therapist in this conversation. If you start uncovering deep traumas, veer off. The goal is to get the Christian's underlying feelings and impressions out in the open where he can begin to see them objectively, not to deal with psychiatric problems.

5. Pursue this line by asking questions that honor the believer's point of view while implicitly stating that there is an alternative. Ask, "Do you think everyone feels this way?" Simply making feelings and impressions explicit is a good way to do this. Do not encourage the believer to intellectualize. Their whole problem is that they don't know how to separate thinking from feeling. Don't confuse the issue.

6. Try to get the believer to see reality in

little pieces. Say, "A lot of innocent children drowned in Katrina," or: "All the gay people I know are very nice and haven't done any harm to anyone." Don't ask a question at this point. Just leave the fact hanging in the air.

7. If the believer falls back on some catch-all defense such as "Katrina was part of God's plan, and we can't comprehend it," don't debate this. Say, "That's one explanation." If you think the believer is ready for a little nudge, then say, "I prefer to see the dead children's point of view."

8. Talk about your own feelings and impressions. If the believer says that there is no meaning without God, say "I see the world as a generally safe place where people can accomplish their goals. I think people are capable of being reasonable and tolerant and generous. I think that the harm that we do each other comes from holding false beliefs." They will know that you mean that one of the harmful false beliefs is religion. You do not need to mention it. You can elicit why the world seems meaningless without God and gently reality test their belief or respond with your own experience. Stay away from arguments for or against God, because you will be talking about the tent, rather than the person within it or the poles holding it up.

9. Once you have gotten the believer's emotional reasons for his belief out in the open, you can

carefully talk about these feelings. Reference yourself mostly. "I feel a kind of belongingness in the universe, too, but it is mostly caused by my belief that I am suited for the world and by my acceptance of things I cannot change. A feeling of belonging doesn't imply that there is a person loving you."

10. Your overall goal here is to get the person to think and feel about reality rather than about their belief system, to develop a perception that is not under the tent, a perception that they can use to leverage real change. You will not persuade them on the spot, but you might set something in motion, and if you are kind, considerate and reasonable, they might come back to you for further discussion. At least they won't be able to dismiss you and your views because you are another rancorous, smart-ass atheist. Remember, your job is to make your point of view attractive to someone who doesn't know how to think.

11. The best way to present yourself to a Christian you are trying to convert is as the happy, serene atheist you are. Never assume you know the individual psychology of the person you're talking to until you've spent a lot of time listening to him or her. Do not condescend. Condescension is an ego satisfaction, and one whiff of an ego satisfying itself will destroy hours of built-up trust.

12. Once you have built up trust and established

a centered way of communicating, you can, if you feel it is appropriate, discuss the traditional arguments for and against the existence of God. But only do so if you have gotten the underlying "tent poles" out in the open enough that the believer can deal with the auxiliary beliefs—the guy wires that help support the tent. At this point they may be his last objections to giving up his belief in God.

The weakness of this approach is that you might get a Christian who says "This is not about my feelings; it's about the reality of God" and who wants to drag the discussion back to arguments in a combative way. If that happens, you might try eliciting that belief in God is based on faith and faith is necessarily based on motives. Even getting your interlocutor to talk about feelings regarding God is still better than talking about arguments, which are largely beside the point if approached in the wrong spirit. If the believer still wants to talk arguments, don't try to back him into a corner. Ask thought-provoking questions and provide your own point-of-view without hectoring.

This approach to discussion verges on therapy, because it bypasses the Christian's official beliefs and gets down to the almost childlike thought/feelings that are the substrate of our lives. But I don't think it crosses the line into inappropriate "treatment" because it doesn't involve delving into childhood traumas or anything like that. It's just two people talking about how they view life. It goes without saying that you should never ever apply a psychiatric label to the person you're talking with. Be careful who you take this approach with, however. If you are talking to someone who is obviously very fragile, angry or rigid, you are probably dealing with someone who has serious emotional issues, and you should not engage him or her. Some people operate on a delicate equilibrium, and you don't want to upset that unless you are asked to do so and you are qualified to help them pick up the pieces if they shatter.

I suspect that some of my readers will misunderstand the approach I have outlined. They will think it subjective, anti-intellectual, even cowardly, because it is non-confrontational. This impression is due to a mistaken idea about the level on which to engage someone whose thought processes are so disarrayed. If your goal is to help someone who lives in a Bubble Universe change his mind, you should not throw abstract arguments at him and confront him with the righteous truth of your side of the issue. You need to meet him on his level, where he's actually making the mistake, and help him peek out of his tent. Notice that your feelings and impressions—your "testimony" and "witnessing"—actually do constitute philosophical premises—it's just that you should put them in easily digested form. I am not proposing an anti-intellectual approach. I am sure many atheists already know what I am saying, but perhaps others do not.

If you're debating a Christian in a public forum, however, a somewhat more confrontational approach may be called for, because it is not him you are trying to convince but the audience. You still owe the person you're debating politeness: no condescension, no *ad hominem,* no genetic fallacy, etc.

Going back to one-on-one discussions, ask yourself,

what would you rather do: change a life or preach at someone who can't really hear you anyway? I think it's braver to reach out to your interlocutor as a human being and expose your personal thoughts and feelings to him.

Your overall goal in this kind of encounter with a Christian is not to win an argument, which you probably can't win anyway, but to get the person you're talking with to notice more of reality, perhaps more of the reality of the world he is blotting out, but definitely more of his internal reality. This is crucial because Christianity, like all voluntary errors, is born of a confusion of the inner world and the outer. The greatest kindness you can show is to gently pull back the tent flaps and let the sunshine in.

The Sleeper Awakes

Ever since I was a child I have been inspired by the idea of greatness. Once I got past the comic book phase of this interest, I turned to adult heroes such as Abraham Lincoln, Atticus Finch and Howard Roark as models. These figures helped shape my understanding of what a human being can and should do.

This set of heroes is instructive, because they are different in so many ways. Their diversity might allow us to get closer to the essence of greatness without getting distracted by merely incidental features shared by examples that are too similar.

What if anything do these three figures have in common, other than that they are all white American males? Let's check on some of the superficial qualities of greatness that they might possess. First, they aren't all geniuses, because Atticus is just a small-town lawyer. Second, they don't all look noble, because Lincoln did not. Third, they are not all rescuers of other people, because Roark is not. Clearly, they do not seem to have in common any of these conventional attributes of greatness.

But there is more to greatness than these superficial qualities. What our three examples have in common is that each is an independent thinker in some key ways, each is centered, each is non-reactive, and each deals with reality instead of fantasy. They may not have been perfect, but they lived in their own skins and did not adopt a false self. They were aware and present, and they were all courageous and perseverant. In short, their greatness lies in their method of consciousness, not their physical, emotional or intellectual enormity.

This kind of greatness is open to everyone. While not everyone has artistic or oratorical genius, everyone *can* learn to be more aware. The other essays in this book have largely been about impediments to awareness. Most of the character types I have been discussing fail to distinguish what's in their heads from what's in reality. Then live in the "reality" they have projected onto existence, rather than seeking the actual world. Such processes of falsified awareness entail self-deception, usually not outright evasion, but a kind that is performed more or less innocently. This type of self-deception is possible because human beings can do things without explicitly knowing that they are doing them.

When I say that people don't entirely know what they're doing, I don't mean to say that people are ruled by the subconscious. Far from it. What I mean is that people do things *implicitly.* For example, we can speak grammatically without knowing the rules of grammar in an overt way. It is not that the unconscious reaches up from the murky depths and pulls our strings when we speak; it's that the rules are embedded and unnamed. With some thought, however, they can be made explicit, systematized and even modified. The basic cause of the kinds of self-deception I wrote about in the other essays is that when we are young we train our mental apparatus without understanding it, and so we end up misusing it. For example, a Pretender adopts a pseudo sense of life usually without knowing what a genuine sense of life is. This behavior is implicit, like the rules of grammar, and thus is not fully under conscious control, unless and until it is made explicit.

Herein lies one of the central problems of human existence: how to use our mighty cognitive apparatus without being choked by its artifacts. Pseudo sense of life, prejudice, religion, a belief in the Zeitgeist, vampire fantasies, fantasies of primalism, rationalism, the Bubble Universe, and so forth are all dysfunctional artifacts of consciousness and they all diminish us, even though they exist only because of reason, which is our highest faculty.

Don't get me wrong: we need artifacts of consciousness. That's what words and numbers are. Art is an artifact. Social institutions such as marriage are. It's not that artifacts as such are bad, it's that by their nature it is easy to create specious ones, ones that obstruct our view of reality rather than enabling it. It is easy because it needs to be easy, because if they are to do their job, the mind's building blocks must be like moveable type that can be freely arranged in any order. This flexibility allows us to put concepts together to make true ideas—but it also allows us to put concepts together to make false ones. This situation calls for philosophy and psychology as a remedy, but explicit philosophy and psychology are latecomers on the scene, and human life did not and could not wait until they caught up to it.

So how can reason be kept on the rails? How can we attain the greatness of great awareness? How can we learn to perceive reality more directly and free from illusions? I would like to offer three solutions to these problems.

Implicit Made Explicit

The first solution I learned from a book: *Focusing* by Eugene Gendlin. This 1982 work by a University of Chicago philosopher and psychotherapist describes a method of making your impressions explicit.

A little background (and I'm putting this more in my own language than in Gendlin's): we all have impressions of things, but most of them are inarticulate. Say that you are shopping for a car and you feel that something is wrong between you and the salesman. You have an impression of his off-putting demeanor. This impression is not an emotion, but a "felt sense," almost like a connotation. The problem is that you don't know why you feel that way. Maybe you're just reacting to the man's oily personality and not to any real dishonesty. Maybe he is doing something shady but you could counter it, if you knew what it was. You don't like the feeling, but you don't want to say something when you don't know what's bothering you. You're stuck and you need more information than your superficial impressions provide you with.

Gendlin would say that you have a deep impression of such situations and that your impression is perceived as an image, a phrase, or a feeling in your throat, chest or belly. He developed a technique wherein you "focus" on it, characterize its sensual quality to your-self, and then use a back-and-forth process of associat-ing and checking to put it into words. There's more to it than that, but that's the basic idea.

Apply the method to the twitchy feeling you get in your chest around the salesman. What does that twitchy feeling feel like? At first it feels like teetering, as if you're off balance. More brainstorming and at-tention to the feeling. Ah yes, it feels as if you're being bowled over—rushed. Does "rushed" cover the feel-ing? Back and forth a couple of times to see whether they match. Then you conclude that they do: the sales-man is using a subtle power play on you. What will probably happen at this point is that the feeling in your chest will give way to a new feeling of resolve, and either you will stop the salesman from rushing you or you will calmly walk away from him. Part of the beauty of the technique is that by making the feelings explicit, you allow them to develop in a healthy way. You become "unstuck" and move on to the next stage, whatever that is. If you get another felt sense, focusing again might help you move further still.

In that example, the felt sense was experienced as a visceral feeling in the torso. Personally, I experience most of my impressions as visual-tactile images. For example, when I thought about the concept of pseudo sense of life just now it was like a thick rubber mat that I was lifting up one edge of to see what's under-neath. This is because I think of pseudo sense of life as an overlay to reality, but one that can be separated from what's under it. Some insights in my life I only understood in a dimly-glimpsed visual-tactile form until I used Gendlin's technique to make them explicit.

You might experience your impressions in yet another way, perhaps as a more purely visual image or as a word or phrase, or who knows what else. The point is you're experiencing your impressions pre-conceptually in some more-or-less concrete form. If you're seriously interested in trying this technique, I strongly recommend using Gendlin's book as a guide, because I am not doing justice to his method. In addition, a site devoted to focusing can be found on the Web.

The experiences we have of our impressions could be regarded as *bodily metaphors*. Gendlin writes about feelings that are sticky or like a heavy ball. I myself sometimes get impressions that look/feel like architectural features such as stairwells and windows and partitions. This form of experience is, Gendlin believes, the interface between the body and the mind. I think it's probable that before we find words for our impressions they usually exist in the form of these bodily metaphors, and that to be a completely integrated and centered person, you have to be aware of this kind of processing and be friendly with it.

Focusing is not an arbiter of truth. Once a felt sense is made explicit, one is in a position to decide whether or not it is accurate, and one does so by a process of reason (and possibly more focusing). One has to be careful in doing this because there is a tendency to dismiss one's non-verbal impressions in favor of one's "official" beliefs or vice versa. Some very analytical people do the former. Some very intuitive people embrace their impressions and never check them against their intellectual knowledge of reality. Don't privilege one over the other. Stay centered, use experience and concepts that you can see for yourself, not preconceptions or learned ideas. Look for the kernel of truth in your feelings and thoughts, and regard conflicts between impressions and explicit beliefs as opportunities to grow.

Let's work through a scenario of a Pretender focusing. Imagine a Cool person is thinking about some Cool objects, such as a pair of shoes. Let's say she tries focusing on her feelings about these objects. Perhaps when she thinks about wearing them, she notices is a feeling of uplift, like a rush in her chest. What is there when she unpacks the feeling? Perhaps an image/feeling of being swept up in a current in the world—of surfing on it, as if she's riding a wave of Cool. If she focuses on the feeling, she may realize that the current is purely within her, not in the world at all, only her personal reaction to a fantasy drawn from her culture, a reaction pumped up by her own hype. If she realizes that, she will have begun to de-mystify her implicit notion of the Zeitgeist. At this point, the impression of Coolness would probably start to collapse. This shift might engender a feeling of disappointment, but it would ultimately lead to a clear, clean feeling of self-awareness because she would no longer be defining reality and herself in terms of a bogus concept. Of course, it would probably take more that just a single act of focusing to fully achieve this insight.

Focusing could profitably be applied to all the forms of self-deception considered in this book. Focusing touches off a series of realizations about the world and how you see it, like walking down a long hallway of doors that open before you. (That's one of my architectural felt senses, by the way.) Notice, however, that it does not much deal in explicit intellectual concepts, but in bodily or imagistic metaphors. It's not philosophy. If you're just trying to figure out why the car salesman is bothering you, this lack of intellectuality might not be a problem, but if you're trying to figure out whether or not abortion is moral, you will need explicit and systematic concepts, too. You can feel your way through a situation only so far without abstractions. Without thinking in concepts too, there is a danger that focusing will just lead you to recycle your existing beliefs.

So focusing won't do everything for you. But what focusing will do, among other things, is help you see that often what you thought was "out there," such as Coolness, is really "in here," and it will give you a first-draft identification of whatever you were thinking about. At the very least, it could provide you with a metaphor you can use as a handle until you arrive at a more explicit identification of your impression.

But focusing isn't just for disillusioning yourself. Returning to the idea of greatness as awareness, I would say that most people have fascinating and unique perceptions of life, if only they could get at them. Sometimes you see these perceptions best in old people, who as they age often seem to lose their inhibitions, not only about expressing a point of view but also about *having* a point of view. But why wait until you're old? You know more than you think you know right now. Gendlin's technique of focusing can help you get at that interesting stuff. I used focusing extensively in the writing of this book.

Presence at the Core

The second idea that can help people reach their peak awareness I call "centering." I don't have one source for the idea but have cobbled it together from things I've learned here and there and from my own experience. I've borrowed the name from certain religious traditions that use it in a somewhat different way from the way I do. You could also call it "presence," a term I employ somewhat differently from its typical use as well. "Centeredness" as I use the term is a mental state in which you both *allow* yourself to be and *cause* yourself to be present in the real world, while shaking off anything that isn't essentially real. "Unreal" things would include ego satisfactions, obsessions, fantasies and other distractions as well as any proxy self or third-person perspective on yourself. Unreal things would also consist of any beliefs you cannot at least intuitively tie back to lived reality. When you center you welcome your grounded perceptions, emotions and bodily feelings and allow them to approach you, to seep into you and to permeate you from within. The essence of centering is to engage the world so that it and you seem fully real and so the usual chatter of false awareness dissipates like mist in the morning sun.

Thus, centering, as I mean it, is a state of mental focus in which one chooses true awareness and sets aside false awareness. Now, it may sound strange to talk about "false awareness." Awareness is awareness, right? Even when you're aware of a falsehood, you're still aware. That's correct, but that's not what I mean. False awareness occurs when one fills one's mind with distractions that act as a screen between oneself and reality--as when one tries to entertain oneself when one should be engaging reality, for example. It's not the same thing as an awareness of a falsehood.

In its most basic form, centering is quite easy to perform: Stop what you're doing and thinking, take a few deep, slow breaths, relax, feel your body, look around—and there you are. Of course, it takes more work than this—you have to really stop the chatter and explore your inner and outer personal space. This exercise won't strip away years of Pretending, but at least for a minute you can cease to engage in obsessing, pleasing others, maintaining a pseudo sense of life, etc. There you are, present in the real world. This is the way in which consciousness achieves its proper relationship to existence, and with practice it can become a stable part of your life.

I might be able to make the concept of centering more intuitive by relating it to an everyday practice. Sometimes when a person has too much going on mentally and starts to be overwhelmed, she stops and "clears her head." When I center, it's something like clearing my head. I recognize that all the things I am thinking about, especially the obsessions and the hyped-up things, are really not part of me. The difference between centering and clearing your head is that the latter usually does not involve letting reality seep into you, but only clears a space. Centering goes an extra step and entails becoming aware of yourself and your surroundings with a profound attitude of serenity so that all the things that would crowd you out of your own head just fall away.

I don't want to make centering sound more passive

than it is. You don't just let the world in; you go out and meet it, discovering it in all its independent glory. Centering as I understand it involves an active practice of wonder. And centering doesn't mean just *being aware* of a self, it means *creating* a fully realized self by choosing to be fully aware and self-aware, concentrating all the diffuse molecules of consciousness into a solid, self-guided person. This is the meaning of presence: when you center, you choose to be fully present in the world, which is fully present to you.

To understand centering, we have to understand the alternative, which is going out of center. When one goes out of center, one is actually trying to lessen awareness. Sometimes one is just letting one's mind go slack by "zoning out," but usually one actively drowns out real awareness by turning up the volume on diverting ideas and mental states. This can include ego satisfactions, TV, obsessive web surfing and gaming, procrastinations, titillations, mystical feelings, etc. It can also include taking a third-person perspective on aspects of your life or participating inappropriately in a group mind as we saw in "Sex and Power, Hugs and Wonder." To be centered is to see the world fundamentally in the first person singular. Only with that foundation can you healthily become part of a "we"; otherwise, being part of a group is just running away from oneself.

An example of an out-of-center person would be the Smart-Ass Pretender. Such a person feels constant pressure to show others that he knows more than they do about the ironic and cynical nature of the world. This is so obviously an attempt to distract himself from his belief in his own defectiveness that it hardly bears mentioning. The Smart-Ass craves attention and tries to steal it because he doesn't know how to get it in a healthy way. His pseudo sense of life shields him from his deeply crest-fallen feelings about himself. He needs to center and use focusing so that he can get at his real issues and stop trying to escape from a situation that in actuality is probably not as bad as he fears.

In this book the biggest diversion from centeredness has been the Pretended sense of life. Where a genuine sense of life is arrived at from a centered position, a Pretended sense of life requires being out of center: It floats untethered like a fantasy. Centering can help you to eliminate pseudo sense of life in two ways: First, it can help you pull back from the false awareness of ego satisfactions, which are what pseudo sense of life is based on. Second, it can help you find the natural tempo of head and heart so that you exit Fast Time and stop skimming over the world.

Racing ahead of your true consciousness is an attempt to overmuch control your experience. Centering, on the other hand, means

listening

to your breathing,

to the breeze rustling the leaves,

to the murmurs of the voices around you,

choosing to be present,

feeling no pressure,

moving with an unrushed heart,

selecting your path with your whole self.

Going out of center by contrast means whistling non-stop to drown out your anxiety as you scuttle down life's desperate alleys.

"Centering," as I use the word, is perhaps similar to the term "mindfulness," as it is used in certain traditions of meditation, although the process by which one achieves it is different, since centering does not involve long stretches of contemplation but is just a way of resetting your mind. Perhaps centering should be looked at as brief form of meditation, lasting from a few seconds to one or two minutes in most cases. I don't know much about the subject, but it seems plausible to me that while some people need extended sessions of meditation, others can get by with several brief resets every day.

I believe that if we center and stop allowing ourselves to be carried along by our preoccupations, we intuitively know what constitutes our core being. The real me is my body, my "life force," the steady hum of my attention, my first-hand realizations, the peace at the heart of me and the love for people and projects that goes all the way down. When I center, I am not "getting in touch" with those things, I am *being* those things. When I am out of center, I drift away from myself and mistake the casual things I think and feel for my self. I skim over the surface of the world, or else I get stuck on some bad feeling, as if it were my whole universe.

Many people who try to stay out of center are afraid of being alone with themselves. If they maintain their pseudo sense of life or other obsessions then they can block out anxiety to some extent. The anxious feelings that provoke Pretending and the other self-distractions, seem, based on my layperson's observations, to be feelings of meaninglessness, helplessness and worthlessness. When such feelings are serious enough, they require therapeutic intervention. But if they are just at the level of life problems, then one might try addressing them oneself, using a technique such as centering, which is useful for helping one fly under anxiety's radar, close to solid ground.

All this might sound as if centering was mere navel-gazing, concerned only with internal processes and living in the now. That is not the case. It's true that centering in my sense means finding calm in the I of life's hurricane. But it also includes an increased awareness of my surroundings and of other people and a grounded connection to the past and the future. When I don't center, things and people in my life can become too much like fantasies, characters in my private story or objects that I see through the lens of my obsessions, annoyance, lust, etc. When I do center, I stop seeing things (including people) primarily through their relationship to my feelings and let them be what they are separate from me. I recognize that things in the world have their own independent existence that doesn't answer to my will. This includes especially the people I love, whom I cannot be said truly to love if I try to control them.

From a centered position, even if I plan to change something in the world or in myself, I still accept it for what it is right now and try to change it in harmony with its nature. I don't fight it or wish it were something else. Instead, I *honor* it, even if I am choosing to annihilate it. Viewed with this attitude, things end up seeming more solid, more present, and more *real.* My love for them becomes cleaner, more sun-lit. My presence in the world and the world's presence to me meet in concord and strength.

Let me be clear: I am not saying that centering will tell you tell you what is true or false, a good value or a bad one—it is no replacement for conceptual reasoning. What I am saying that centering will pull you back from what you are using to distract yourself and let you be who you really are. When you pare away the distractions, you are left with, not a *perfect* self, but a more *authentic* self that can use principles, observations, felt senses and the ideas of others to seek out truth and goodness. And they do have to be sought out. We aren't perfect or complete underneath our inauthenticities: We are naturally unformed, and if we are not careful, we end up malformed. As I discussed in "Sex and Power, Hugs and Wonder," proper values grow in conjunction with reason, although I would add that it is with a robust reason, that makes use of the unconscious, focusing in Gendlin's sense of the term, and emotions, not a geometric or Mr. Spock kind of reason.

Most people are not going to stay for very long in a deeply centered state just by "clearing their head." The problems and obsessions that distract one from attaining one's true greatness will not permanently dissolve in the liquid of centering. No, one needs further techniques and ideas. This is where practices such as focusing in Gendlin's sense come in. Focusing can help you identify your obsessions and distractions one by one and get unstuck, making it easier to stay in a centered state. Then you can scrutinize your thinking and get past the feelings of meaninglessness, helplessness and worthlessness that lead you to Pretend, drink, believe in God, etc. You end up realizing that you are alive and serenely glad of it, that you've got resources and possibilities, and that things are not as dire (or even as boring) as they seemed. You can engage the world and other people and are ready to form more realistic plans and address your problems, whatever they are.

I'm not saying, though, that you should be in a highly individuated state such as centering all the time. We should lose ourselves in passion, in music, in our work, in feeling a connection with the cosmos. Ecstasy and flow states are not false awareness, even though they do not entail the same kind of intense self-perception as we get in centering. It would be wrong to prescribe one state of consciousness for human beings in all situations. But I would regard the centered, focused state as the baseline for healthy human functioning.

The Reality Principle

Earlier I mentioned that I'd like to offer three ideas for getting more in touch with reality and achieving the greatness of increased awareness. Gendlin's focusing technique was the first idea. Centering was the second. The third is a way of looking at the world mentioned earlier in the book: Ayn Rand's concept of the Primacy of Existence.

The name means that existence (the external world) comes before consciousness (the internal world). You could label this concept the "Reality Principle." According to this way of looking at things, there is a world out there that is what it is, regardless of what we think of it, and that cannot be affected by mere wishes. According to the Primacy of Existence, if we want to get something done we have to look out at reality, discover its nature and act appropriately, not look inward and hope. In other words we need to treat reality according to its rules instead of trying to impose our own on it. For example, a college student practices the Reality Principle studies by taking notes, doing research, making flashcards, etc.—she does not imagine that she will get an *A* just by thinking positive thoughts.

The Primacy of Existence makes a clean distinction between the outer world and the inner. It holds that the world is separate from and independent of the mind. Without the Reality Principle as at least an implicit guide, people tend to treat external reality as an extension of the self. Mental pre-occupations, such as the pseudo sense of life of the Pretender, the Zeitgeist of the Cool, the fantasies of the primalists, etc. appear to be objective because one is allowing one's feelings and wishes to slop over onto one's perception of reality. One ends up seeing them as quasi-spiritual qualities in the world, as a tone or a vibe or a groove. According to the Primacy of Existence, however, the mind is dependent on external reality for its contents, and the world outside the self (i.e. outside of the conscious, bodily person) is unaffected by thoughts and feelings, unless those thoughts and feelings are realized in bodily action.

You might think that everyone is naturally focused on reality, that it's like breathing, but nothing could be further from the truth. I remember a joke from the 1960s: "Reality is just a crutch for people who can't handle drugs." Many people actually think this way, and not just about drugs. All the problematic personality types considered in this book, including Pretenders, Cool people, vampire lovers, drinkers and serious Christians, to some extent reject the Reality Principle. They believe implicitly in the opposite notion, which Rand called the Primacy of Consciousness. You could term this the "Wishing-Makes-It-So Principle." This false premise blurs the line between the mind and the world and says that we can affect or even create reality by mere feeling. It is the basis of all supernaturalist and magical thinking. Throughout this book we have been considering people who believe that they can re-shape the universe through the power of fantasy. They are trying to flee into a realm in which sense of life, style, feelings, etc. are thought of as in the air around us, rather than as things that exist only within us.

Since sense of life has been our principal concept in this book, let's compare the genuine sense of life of the authentic person to the pseudo sense of life of the Pretender to see how our opposing principles play out: A genuine sense of life is arrived at by a process of exploring the world and one's place in it. A pseudo sense of life is arrived at by a process of adopting an attitude and projecting fantasy feelings onto the world. A genuine sense of life is organic and rich. A pseudo sense of life is contrived and simplistic. A genuine sense of life grows out of being centered. A pseudo sense of life comes from being out of center. To sum up, the authentic person makes a self by engaging the world; the Pretender tries to re-make the world in his own image and to create an identity without going through the work of discovering what the world offers.

People who believe in the Primacy of Consciousness tend to think that they can do whatever they want with their minds, that they can become who they want to be just by acting and feeling a certain way. But even the self has an objective identity that cannot be changed by snapping one's fingers. To be sure, you do control many things in your life, but if you want to become a different person, you have to go through a sometimes-difficult process of re-examining your beliefs, feelings and behaviors. You may need to revisit the choices and impressions that you based your life on—including the big, deep choice of a adopting a pseudo sense of life. If you stay centered, use focusing and remain true to reality, you can achieve an authentic changed self. But if you only adopt an attitude and a few new habits and fashions, you will just become a Teddy Roosevelt style of Pretender. It's not enough to want to be different: You have to honor your own soul just as much as you would honor the identity of a material object you wished to change—and change it according to its nature.

Most of the character types we have examined in this book are Pretenders who practice the Primacy of Consciousness. The Fast-Time Pretender wants to impart emotional torque to reality to rev it up to his hyped velocity. The vampire lover uses horrific stories to conjure a dark fantasy world that supports the out-of-context romantic feelings she wishes to support. Cool people summon the Zeitgeist, a quasi-spiritual construct consisting of their reified sense of style. The primalist substitutes a fantasy complex of hasty conclusions, media role models, and personal dreams for solid thinking about the world. Drinkers, needless to say, think they can change reality just by changing their mental states. All of these strategies assist the various Pretender types in their attempt to live in the world they want to live in rather than in the world that is.

Serious believers in God, although often more complex than Pretenders, also embrace the Primacy of Consciousness, in two ways: first, they use faith (which is a form of fantasy) to create a mythological Bubble Universe that they put between themselves and reality; second, they invent a free-floating mind (i.e. a god) that has the power to affect reality at will, thereby putting reality at the mercy of a pure spirit, which is the Primacy of Consciousness writ large.

Of course, almost no one is so bold as to say that something is real just because they want it to be, although Pollyanna Pretenders come close, and religious folk say that things are real just because God wants them to be, which is the same principle. But leaving aside these extreme cases, what believers in the primacy of consciousness usually do is to project their mental constructs onto reality and then believe they found them there, mixing up mind and world into a messy soup of wishful thinking. This isn't the same as making up one's own facts (as in "My co-worker really digs me.")—it's worse. At least facts are a real category and can be checked. Disembodied sense of life "auras" or Zeitgeists or spirits are never going to be real, no matter what details one fills in, and when people go to "check" them, they almost invariably consult their feelings rather than reality.

This is in no way intended to denigrate feelings. Feelings are a dimension of experience without which life would be not only unbearable but also impossible, because we need them in order to experience values, form and execute plans, and help discover the truth. However, the importance of feelings does not change the fact that reality is just not imbued with feeling. The world consists of people, other living beings and things like rocks and stars—that's all. Sense of life, will, fantasy—those are entirely within us; they do not exist outside of us. Projecting one's feelings onto the world is a deadly mistake because it leads one to turn away from the real world in favor of mental phantoms. It's like driving while watching television—and is about as successful.

People typically substitute feelings for facts because they have never learned how to use their minds or because they are afraid of certain facts. This is sad, because, speaking broadly, we are evolved to live in this world. We are suited to it. It is lawful and we can, up to our biological limits, be effective in it as long as we use reason. I would go so far as to say that the world is a fitting object of our love. But we should not kid ourselves that the world loves us back or that it comes with soundtrack music in the form of external sense of life emotions. The right way to see the world is as an immense collection of opportunities, all governed by natural law. And the right way to see ourselves is as living gems amidst all that vastness, giving it meaning.

This whole book represents an exploration of the Primacy of Consciousness in the many ways it has come to pervade American life—and its remedy, the Primacy of Existence. (For more on these principles, see Ayn Rand's essay, "The Metaphysical vs. the Man-Made" in her collection *Philosophy: Who Needs It.*)

These concepts are the fundamental alternative that divides good ideas, like those of Aristotle and the Enlightenment from bad ones, like those of religion and modernism. The Enlightenment's emphasis on the Primacy of Existence, imperfect as it was, shaped America in its early years. But the influence of religious revivals, Hegel, Emerson, the social Darwinists and the pragmatists turned the nation toward the Primacy of Consciousness.

Now young people have virtually no philosophical guidance and desperately reach for vampire stories, Coolness and God as substitutes, since they have been taught by modern philosophy that everything is a matter of arbitrary "commitment" anyway—meaning that whatever they choose to follow is just as good as anything anyone else chooses, and no one can tell them they are wrong. Just when young people need guidance most, our culture places an abyss in their path. Their bravery before this abyss is admirable, even if many of their choices are not. However, their bravery is sad because it is needless, since the world is real, life is real and other people are real: Among these real things we can find a morality that is not arbitrary, but is instead objective—and glorious—a morality based on life on this wonderful planet of ours.

The Primacy of Existence is the foundation of a fully secular, naturalistic worldview. If you use the Primacy of Existence to distinguish between the mind and reality, you can slash off whole categories of errors, because by referring to it we know that some things simply aren't real. Feelings and will do not exist free-floating in the universe; therefore, Pretenderism, Zeitgeist, karma, luck, God and primalist fantasies have no foundation in reality. These things are only echoes of our own minds.

Some people might feel that the secular way of looking at the world I describe is sterile and that I am robbing the world of its enchantment. Not so. The ocean, a skyscraper, a child—all are just as beautiful to me without illusions as they would be with. Actually, they are *more* beautiful, because I am not overlaying them with the musty and misplaced artifacts of a fevered imagination. They do not require extra help to be beautiful. They are beautiful because life is beautiful. My life. Yours.

Conclusion

My goal in this essay has been to share three ideas that could help the reader achieve the greatness of figures like Abraham Lincoln, Howard Roark and Atticus Finch, a greatness based on increased awareness, attainable by anyone. Focusing helps us discover what is within us; centering helps us become one with our true perceptions of self and reality; and the Primacy of Existence helps us separate reality from fantasy. Making the positive ideas discussed in this essay and throughout this book second nature could make it possible for the reader to live more in the real world and find the joy that comes from dealing with reality, including other human beings.

Forming, or re-forming, these habits of mind can also help America solve the cultural problems mentioned in the Introduction and throughout the book. Most obviously, they can help us beat back Pretenderism, which would lessen the temptation to go on crusades foreign and domestic: We will give up crisis thinking and stop casting ourselves in the role of rescuer. They would help us to be more realistic in our economic activities and to avoid the "irrational exuberance" that comes with rationalism. They could help people get in touch with real values, so that they were less tempted by the meretricious enticements of Cool, including smoking, drugs and corrosive irony. They could help people see through religion, scientism and all other faith-based beliefs. And they could improve the tone of everyday life as our obsessions with gore and snarkiness recede. With a rational philosophy growing in the soil prepared by these habits of mind, America would start to reclaim its heritage as a nation of common sense, good will and practicality, governed by the principles of Liberty and Equality, which are the political implications of reason. We would once again become a nation of builders, instead of a nation of consumers and couch potatoes.

A resurgence of reason would be an immense boon to American culture, but the most salutary *interpersonal* effect of the Primacy of Existence, focusing and centering is that they would help us see other people as real. If you recognize that others are real beings separate from you, rather than mere characters in your fantasy to be mocked or romanticized, it is harder to be cruel to them or to make idols of them or to violate their rights, and of course you will get much more out of knowing them. I won't go so far as to say that you will love everybody—I've never seen how one is supposed to love bad people or even people who might be good but whom one does not know, except in a diffuse "all men are brothers" kind of way. But seeing other people as real will lead you to look for and sympathize with the unique problems that life has given each of us to solve—and you will perceive in each person's solution a unique humanity. You will look in their eyes and see, not a mirror, but a bottomless well of presence to match your own.

The habits of mind we have been discussing can, of course, aid the individual in and of himself as well. By achieving presence, you can live as a real self in the real world, rather than as a Cool character in a Cool world, a servant of God in God's world, etc. With these tools you can become what may seem paradoxical to some: serene yet passionate, matter-of-fact yet spiritual, and contemplative yet dynamic. You can become a solid being grounded in the earth rather than a self made of shadows. You can realize the ideal of greatness as awareness I began this essay with. This is the culmination of what I called "concrete ethics" in the Introduction.

These tools will empower you to take responsibility for your feelings, because you will recognize that they are yours and not the world's. And these tools will free you from hype, which is the poison of our age, by helping you find peace at the center. Furthermore, realizing that there is no cosmic consciousness will help you regard each real consciousness as more precious, because you will see, first, that the individual is not a puppet of some illusory outside force, and second, that each of us by our very existence is a fount of meaning in the universe. That is a marvel far superior to any that religion has to offer.

Pretenderism and the rest are basically superstitions. Every move in history away from superstition has traumatized some people and led them to long for what was left behind. Yet enlightenment has always brought a better way of living. What did Charles Darwin say about his theory of natural selection? "There is grandeur in this view of life." I would say the same thing about the view that I espouse. If you accept it, you get to see the world for what it is: a realm you can understand, admire and shape, a sovereign domain free from the capricious interventions of God and Mr. Murphy. Furthermore, each of us gets to be what we really are: an incredible assemblage of abilities striving to actualize themselves, rather than a disjointed false self racing to keep up with relics of the mind such as Cool.

For greatness to be realized, we need to live in reality and become ourselves. To do those things, we need to give up our ungrounded beliefs, self-indulgent fantasies and pseudo sense of life. Then we can thoughtfully develop true beliefs, engage in the dreams that will help us get things done, and discover what is amazing and poignant in life—all of which we will do by connecting to the real world and to other people directly. We should stop trying to make reality what it is not just as we should stop trying to make ourselves what we are not. We should abandon our pretensions, our self-deceptions and our false selves, and embrace the world. Then we can live as the beings of passionate wonder we really are.

Postscript: Dirk

I once read a theory that held that the art and music we love tell the world who we are. An opportunity once arose for me to put this theory to the test. I used to know a musician named Dirk Douglas, who died unexpectedly in June 2000. His mother, familiar with my interest in music, gave me his entire CD library. I don't think he'd mind if I spoke frankly, even bluntly, about the lessons I have learned from studying his collection; I knew Dirk for many years, and candor was one of his highest values. Besides, he loved attention.

Dirk had surprisingly narrow affinities. At least 75% of his collection, which numbered 72 discs, came from the 1970s or from bands whose heyday was in the '70s. (Dirk was born in 1954 and so turned 16 in 1970.) He had five or six albums each by Kansas and Yes, as well as greatest hits albums by Foreigner, Starship and the like. He also had a few greatest hits discs from early '80s performers such as Kenny Loggins who were essentially holdovers from the '70s. He had almost no classic 60s rock — an album of Blood, Sweat and Tears from his own brass-band days was about it. He did have a few more recent discs: one by Tori Amos, one by Joan Osborne. He also had several upbeat white gospel albums of recent vintage, presumably acquired during the last few years of his life when his health was poor and he once again turned to Christianity after years of what can only be described as paganism.

There were a few classical and jazz items. Dirk's mother loved Chopin and encouraged Dirk's piano playing. (Dirk was a keyboard player, singer and arranger.) So there was a disc of Chopin performed by Vladimir Horowitz, a soundtrack from the movie "Shine" and one or two "Great Classical Piano Works" compilations. The principle behind his jazz collection I cannot discern, but he did have the good taste to like classic jazz such as Miles Davis' "Kind of Blue" and not modern pop-jazz such as Kenny G.

It is obvious that Dirk favored keyboards, but he also liked vocal harmonies. He had a couple of CDs he'd burned himself featuring songs with tight harmonies. He had greatest hits albums by Queen and Earth, Wind and Fire (among the rare black performers in Dirk's catalogue). Dirk himself had a good, versatile voice, and was not only very proud of his harmonizing but was also a connoisseur of other people's. I remember him explaining to me almost 35 years ago how the Wilson brothers of the Beach Boys and Freddie Mercury of Queen worked their magic. (Sixty-four little Freddies each singing his over-dubbed part in "Bohemian Rhapsody.")

It should be clear that Dirk's musical taste followed his professional interests with regard to the technical dimension. I suspect this is a common correlation among musicians. But there are plenty of musical acts that employ keyboards and/or tight vocals harmonies. Why did

Dirk pick the ones he did?

Dirk started trying to make it as a pro when he was 17, in 1972. He attended a community college but only for a year or so. Despite his impressive intelligence, his formal education in music and everything else ended in the early '70s. The '70s was Dirk's era: he liked the questioning of authority, the sexual freedom, the flamboyance of attire and hairstyle and the drugs.

It is my belief that Dirk was so at home in this era, that he simply stopped growing when it ended. It's common for people's tastes (and beliefs) to harden once they get past college age, especially if drugs are a part of their life. Dirk ceased being of college age around 1976. To be sure, he did still follow trends after 1976, but not ones that *started* after 1976. And this means that he missed out on punk and new wave. Whatever you want to say about punk, it did purge pop music of some of its self-indulgent excesses and made it possible for something ironic and worldly-wise to grow. But there was nothing like the Clash, Elvis Costello or Squeeze in Dirk's collection.

And Dirk's limited taste was reflected in the music he wrote and performed too. The boy was simply lost in the '70s, and that fact, along with his difficult personality and health problems, no doubt accounted for his failure to make it as a musician.

But even this biographical analysis does not peg Dirk and his tastes. If he was so in love with the 70s why didn't he own any Eagles or ELO? Here we need to appeal to Dirk's sense of life and cognitive style. Dirk left an indelible impression on those around him with the way he thought and felt. Let me try to weave an image of Dirk, with the music he owned as the warp and my personal recollections as the woof.

The groups most represented in his collection were Yes and Kansas. What they have in common, other than the obvious, is that both use keyboards as their foundation, both are "hyper" or strident in their pacing and emotional tone, both have pretensions to the "lyrical." The main point of difference is that Yes is more impersonal and arty where Kansas is more intimate and "sincere."

From knowing him, I would say that the decisive element shared by most of the bands in Dirk's collection was "sincerity." Dirk hit his teens in the late '60s, and while he was not a "60s person," he was one of that era's many heirs. Those of you old enough to remember the '70s or who have studied it have surely gleaned that one of its key concepts was "naturalness." Partly this was due to the ecology movement, and partly it was due to the 1960s rejection of process in favor of immediate, "authentic" action, experience and emotion. Put these two influences together, and you get a worship of human nature conceived of as bodily functions and spontaneous feelings. According to this "code of the natural," either you acknowledged those functions and feelings or you futilely tried to deny them. (I remember a poster from the era that yelled, "If it smells good, eat it!") Dirk's attitude towards what was "natural" ranged from matter-of-fact candor to outright wallowing. In short, if Dirk had an itch, he would scratch it–sometimes in public.

Dirk was a primalist, basically of the child variety. Lest I sound one-sidedly critical of Dirk's primalism, let me say that it made him a frank and open person, bolstered his sense of humor (because it helped him puncture people's pretensions), and contributed to his pro-sex attitudes. I have heard from women he was with that he was a wonderful lover. That having been said, I hope it's obvious that I do not take Dirk's beliefs at face value – and that I don't blame him for widespread errors of the culture.

The attitude of "sincerity" and "naturalness" is clearly reflected in Dirk's music. As I write, I am listening to his copy of "Starship: Greatest Hits (Ten Years and Change 1979-1991)." For those of you who don't know, Starship was the successor group to Jefferson Starship, which was in turn the successor to Jefferson Airplane. Each successor represents a diminution of its predecessor. The original Airplane was a band of wild talents fronted by two amazing vocalists, Grace Slick and Marty Balin. Starship was fronted by a third-generation clone of Marty Balin, a histrionic little man named Mickey Thomas, with Grace Slick as little more than a back-up vocalist.

If Starship has one salient quality, it's a loudly-proclaimed earnestness. With his trademark wail, Thomas squeezes every ounce of feeling out of songs such as "Jane," "Sara" and "Nothing's Gonna Stop Us Now," the last of which, improbably, seems to be intended as a wedding anthem for the trailer set. Now I could see a completist fan of the Airplane in all its incarnations buying such a disc, but Dirk didn't own anything by Jefferson Airplane or Jefferson Starship. He headed straight for the trough of emotion that is just plain Starship. This album is a particularly clear reflection of Dirk's values.

With the concept of "naturalness," we have a pretty good hold on Dirk's ethos, but what about his cognitive style? This is somewhat harder to identify, but again his music can be of assistance, especially a group such as Yes.

What distinguishes Yes is its motor-like, almost impersonal drive and complexity. I don't think it's the impersonality as such that attracted Dirk, since most of his collection was anything but impersonal. Rather, it would seem to be the motor-like drive and the complexity. (Think of the paradigmatic Yes song "Roundabout.") These qualities are shared by Kansas (think of the relentless Bach-like piano of "Carry On Wayward Son"). Starship and some of Dirk's other discs also share them to a lesser degree.

There are three reasons why Dirk and the strident style were made for each other. The first is that naturalism in the '70s frequently took an assertive, theatrical cast. (Dirk was largely indifferent to "mellow" groups such as Bread.)

The second is Dirk's personality. Dirk was clinically hyperactive and a melodramatic Pretender. Truth be told, when Dirk was "up" it was difficult to share a room with him.

The third and most relevant is Dirk was a serious showoff. Dirk loved fast, driving, intricate, prestidigitation in music. I call the resulting pseudo sense of life "Razzle-Dazzle." Music with this quality impressed Dirk by attracting the listener's attention and then almost losing it along the way, like a game of three-card monty. Razzle-Dazzle represents the energy and enthusiasm Dirk loved and had in his own life. And Dirk would have liked it that I chose a colloquial term, since he generally believed that a technical or orderly approach to a subject was mere pomposity, a sin he clearly thought that I with my analytic ways was frequently guilty of. Razzle-Dazzle may help explain why Dirk gravitated toward synthesizers and the like, when he was also proficient on piano, guitar, drums and brass instruments: the gee-whiz, high-tech factor appealed to the fast-talking showman in him.

In loving Yes or Kansas or Kenny Loggins, what Dirk

loved was his own feeling that he could bop through the world, getting by on his (pseudo) sense of life. His love of complexity was not primarily about a Bach-like adoration of some crystalline aspect of the universe; it was always about asserting his own personality. He was trying to impress, and the person he sought most to impress was himself.

The history of Dirk's beliefs confirms this analysis: Throughout his various ideological phases, whether he was a born-again Christian, a free-flowing mystic, or a semi-rational student of psychology (à *la* Myers-Briggs), behind it all was always Dirk, the prodigy whose smarts and intuition could discern the truth and deal with it, not by submission to something external (such as reality or even God), but by sheer panache. In many ways Dirk was the emblematic man of the 1970s, a time where naturalness met irony, and technological innovation met earthiness. You could tell by the way he used his walk.

Now we are able to integrate what we know about Dirk's music with what we know about Dirk. The linchpin is an intelligent yet narrow subjectivism. Dirk had a concept of feelings as the ultimate authority and of conjuring the right "groove" as the proper method for success. For him style, or what I am calling pseudo sense of life, was everything. His Pretenderism was archetypal.

And thus it was he failed. Not in a glorious battle with the forces of mediocrity and conformity that he loved to fight, but in sad loneliness. Botched back surgery and a low tolerance for pain (no doubt exacerbated by decades of drug abuse) led him to disability and to dependence on prescription medicine. The damaged woman with whom he had traded emotional support for financial support had died. His father, who had helped get him on public assistance and provided some emotional sustenance when he was disabled, had died. Most importantly, even Dirk could surely see that finally his dreams had died.

One morning in June of 2000, the nurse who helped Dirk with his morphine patches found him dead. He had six of the patches on him and over 100 barbiturate tablets in him. Whether as his friends believe, it was an accidental overdose with pill after pill being taken in a daze, or, as his family believes, it was a suicide, will never be determined with certainty. There was no note.

I don't admire subjectivism, and I know it doesn't work. But I do have to respect Dirk, subjectivism and all. Misguided and crazy as he was his whole life, he did have a dream and he did pursue it. I am reminded of a song from Dirk's collection, perhaps not so atypical as it first may appear to be: "Deacon Blues" by Steely Dan. The song tells the mythic tale of a young man who goes from being a "nobody" to being a jazz musician, very much "in the life." The narrator has such a pre-programmed vision of his own legend that he even predicts that he's going to "die behind the wheel," presumably driving drunk. Yet he concludes:

> This brother is free.
> I'll be what I want to be.

I've always loved the twisted perseverance of that song, and I guess that's how it was possible for me to love Dirk.

So apparently you can tell something about someone by his musical taste, or at least you can use those tastes as a magnifying glass.

Don't let my clinical attitude fool you. I saw through

Dirk, better than anyone else did maybe, but I was not immune to his charms. Dirk's life and death have a greater hold on me than I would ever choose to give them. For you see, "Dirk Douglas" was a stage name that Dirk took as his legal name a decade before he died. His given name was Dirk Douglas Keefner, and he was my older brother. Perhaps I understand his brilliance and his madness because they are partly mine as well. For the rest of my life Dirk will have the power to tear me in two, as I laud his intelligence, talent and decency, loathe his self-indulgence and character flaws and lament his blind spots and drug abuse. In many ways as a child I defined myself against him. No matter how I agonize over his memory, however, I will always be grateful to him for helping to kindle the love of music in me. It is a gift that can never die. I began this book with Dirk; it is only fair that I end it with him.

Now forgive me, gentle reader, for the deception of not revealing my true relation to Dirk sooner. The only way I could stand to write about him when the memory of him still burns and the only way I could adopt a suitably detached tone, is by sending in an impersonal Proxy Self to do the talking for me. Dirk would have enjoyed the gag.

Bibliography

Berne, Eric, *Games People Play: The Psychology of Human Relationships.* New York, Grove Press, 1964.

Bloom, Allan, *The Closing of the American Mind: How Higher Education has Failed Democracy and Impoverished the Souls of Today's Students*, New York, Simon and Schuster, 1987.

Byrne, Rhonda, *The Secret*, New York, Simon and Schuster, 2006.

Branden, Nathaniel, *The Psychology of Self-Esteem: A New Concept of Man's Psychological Nature*, Los Angeles, Nash Publishing, 1969.

Carr, Nicholas, *The Shallows: What the Internet is Doing to our Brains*, New York, W.W. Norton, 2010.

Darwin, Charles, *On the Origin of Species by Means of Natural Selection, or Preservation of Favoured Races in the Struggle for Life*, London, John Murray, 1859.

Dawkins, Richard, *The Selfish Gene*, London, Oxford University Press, 1976.

Dewey, John, *Freedom and Culture*, New York, G.P. Putnam's Sons, 1939.

Fromm, Erich, *The Sane Society*, New York, Rinehart, 1955.

Gendlin, Eugene, *Focusing*, New York, Everest House, 1978.

Gladwell, Malcolm, "The Coolhunt," http://gladwell.com/the-coolhunt/, 1997.

Hill, Napoleon, *Think and Grow Rich*, Cleveland, The Ralston Society, 1937.

James, William, "The Meaning of Truth" in *William James: Writings 1902-1910,* Library of America, 1988.

Keefner, Kurt, *Free Will: A Response to Sam Harris*, available on Kindle, 2012

Lee, Harper, *To Kill a Mockingbird*, Philadelphia, Lippincott, 1960.

Lewis, C. S., *The Abolition of Man ; or, Reflections on Education with Special Reference to the Teaching of English in the Upper Forms of Schools*, New York, Macmillan, 1947.

Marcuse, Herbert, *Eros and Civilization: A Philosophical Inquiry into Freud*, Vintage Books, 1955.

Maslow, Abraham, "A Theory of Human Motivation," 1943, http://psychclassics.yorku.ca/Maslow/motivation.htm

Pettegrew, John. *Brutes in Suits: Male Sensibility in America, 1890-1920*, Baltimore: Johns Hopkins Univ. Press, 2007.

Porter, Eleanor H., *Pollyanna,* L.C. Page, 1913.

Rand, Ayn, *The Fountainhead,* Indianapolis, Bobbs-Merrill, 1943.

Rand, Ayn, *Philosophy: Who Needs It,* Indianapolis, Bobbs-Merrill, 1982.

Rand, Ayn, *The Romantic Manifesto: A Philosophy of Literature,* New York, World Pub. Co., 1969.

Rice, Anne, *Interview with the Vampire,* New York, Alfred A. Knopf, 1976.

Seabury, David, *The Art of Selfishness,* New York, Pocket Books, 1974, originally 1937.

Spitz, Marc, *Twee: The Gentle Revolution in Music, Books, Television, Fashion and Film,* New York, HarperCollins, 2014.

Steiner, Claude, *Games Alcoholics Play,* New York, Grove Press, 1971.

Stoker, Bram, *Dracula,* Archibald Constable and Company, 1897.

Tallis, Raymond, *Aping Mankind: Neuromania, Darwinitis and the Misrepresentation of Humanity,* Durham, England, Acumen Pub., 2011.

Thornhill, Randy and Craig T. Palmer, *A Natural History of Rape: Biological Bases of Sexual Coercion,* Cambridge, Mass. MIT Press, 2000.

Twain, Mark, *Adventures of Huckleberry Finn*, Chatto and Windus, 1884 (UK), Charles L. Webster & Co. 1885 (US).

Twenge, Jean M. and W. Keith Campbell, *The Narcissism Epidemic: Living in the Age of Entitlement,* New York, Simon and Schuster, 2010.

Wilson, Edward O., *Sociobiology: The New Synthesis,* Cambridge, Mass, Harvard UP, 1975.

Acknowledgements

I would like to thank the people who helped me with this book. Phil Schneider gave me constructive feedback and prodded me to add "Justin." Diane D. Baksys and Roger E. Bissell went over the manuscript in great detail, ferreting out many a dangling modifier. My friends on Facebook came up with suggestions when I was stuck for examples. But the biggest debt I owe is to my wife Stephanie Allen. She read many versions of these essays over the course of several years, pushing me to re-write again and again until I developed a style appropriate for my intended audience. Without her, words would truly fail me.

Cover design by Deana Riddle
Photos by Daniel Bottner

ABOUT THE AUTHOR

Kurt Keefner is originally from Springfield, Illinois, and studied philosophy at the University of Chicago. He lives in a Maryland suburb of Washington, DC, with his wife, the author Stephanie Allen. He has published many essays and book and CD reviews, as well as the booklet "Free Will: A Response to Sam Harris," available on Kindle. This is his first full-length work. His blog, "Become Who You Are," is at www.kurtkeefner. com and he can be contacted at keefner.books@hot-mail.com.

www.ingramcontent.com/pod-product-compliance
Lightning Source LLC
Chambersburg PA
CBHW060447280326
41933CB00014B/2692

* 9 7 8 0 6 9 2 2 5 2 5 2 9 *